Promoting
Independent
Media

Promoting Independent Media

Strategies for Democracy Assistance

Krishna Kumar

LYNNE
RIENNER
PUBLISHERS

BOULDER
LONDON

Published in the United States of America in 2006 by
Lynne Rienner Publishers, Inc.
1800 30th Street, Boulder, Colorado 80301
www.rienner.com

and in the United Kingdom by
Lynne Rienner Publishers, Inc.
3 Henrietta Street, Covent Garden, London WC2E 8LU

Library of Congress Cataloging-in-Publication Data
Kumar, Krishna.
Promoting independent media : strategies for democracy assistance /
    Krishna Kumar.
        p. cm.
    Includes bibliographical references and index.
    ISBN 1-58826-429-7 (hardcover : alk. paper)
    1. Mass media—Political aspects. 2. Democracy. I. Title.
P95.8.K86 2006
302.23—dc22   2005029742

British Cataloguing in Publication Data
A Cataloguing in Publication record for this book
is available from the British Library.

Printed and bound in the United States of America

The paper used in this publication meets the requirements
of the American National Standard for Permanence of
Paper for Printed Library Materials Z39.48-1992.

5 4 3 2 1

Contents

Foreword

The media development sector is arguably the most important but least recognized social change movement in the world today. Krishna Kumar's *Promoting Independent Media: Strategies for Democracy Assistance* offers the first serious description and analysis of this burgeoning field. Its publication comes at a propitious moment, as Western governments and foundations are ramping up their support for indigenous media outlets and the local and international NGOs that support them, while authoritarian governments increasingly are clamping down. The seminal role played by independent broadcasters in mobilizing populations to overthrow repressive regimes in Georgia, Kyrgyzstan, Ukraine, and Lebanon have frightened some of their neighbors and raised the stakes for media NGOs. The rise of regional satellite channels like Al Jazeera also is forcing governments to consider wholesale reform of their media's "enabling environments."

This important book examines the most significant examples of media development work to date—in Russia, Bosnia, Serbia, Indonesia, Afghanistan, and Sierra Leone. Each case study reveals different aspects of media development strategies in a variety of political contexts—from hostile, repressive governments to newly democratic ones. The book covers the wide range of media development activities—training, production, distribution, legal and regulatory reform—for radio, television, and print. It makes a strong case for protecting the development of independent media from its voracious cousin, public diplomacy. Media development seeks to expand locally produced indigenous content, and Kumar is correct in warning of any encroachment by those with a message to sell. *Promoting Independent Media* highlights some remarkable successes and regrettable failures and along the way provides an invaluable institutional memory for the sector as a whole.

Policymakers in multilateral and bilateral donor agencies, media NGOs, and civil society organizations engaged in democracy assistance will profit from the book's critical but constructive analysis. Media educators will also find it highly useful for informing journalists about international efforts to promote independent media. Last but not least, all those who cherish freedom of the press and value the unfettered flow of information and ideas will find the book highly informative and thought provoking.

—David Hoffman
President, Internews Network

Preface

Since the late 1980s, the international donor community has provided assistance to postconflict and transition societies to develop and strengthen independent media. The objective of such assistance has been to promote democratization and help lay the foundations for transparent and accountable political institutions. Media assistance is based on the well-founded premise that without a robust media—free of government control and able to sustain itself through sales and advertising—a democratic political order cannot exist. A free media is the lifeblood of democracy.

By the end of 2003, the international community had spent between $600 million and $1 billion on media assistance programs. Most assistance went to the Balkans, Eastern Europe, and Eurasia. Central America and Southern Africa also received a modest share. There is now a perceptible shift of focus from the former communist bloc in Eastern Europe to other regions in Asia and Africa that offer fresh challenges. International donors are designing innovative programs to enlarge the space for independent electronic and print media in Middle Eastern countries.

The substantive focus of media assistance programs has varied, depending on the targeted country, the timing, and the donor. Broadly speaking, the international community has supported a wide array of programs that focus on improving journalistic skills and expertise, promoting the economic viability of media enterprises, sustaining media entities through financial and commodity assistance, promoting legal and regulatory reforms, strengthening the institutional infrastructure for media, and promoting the transformation of the state-owned media.

In this volume, I address questions on the role of international assistance in promoting independent media: What is the nature of media assistance? How is it being delivered? Who are the major actors? What type of programs has the international community supported? What have been media program achievements and shortcomings? And what can be done to improve the effectiveness and impact of media assistance? In answering these questions, I present case studies of media programs in Afghanistan, Bosnia, Central America, Indonesia, Russia, Serbia, and Sierra Leone.

* * *

Several friends have helped me in writing this book. I particularly wish to acknowledge my debt to Zoey Breslar, Peter Graves, Mark Koenig, John Langlois, and Rick Marshall. I am grateful to Dan De Luce for reading the entire manuscript and making invaluable suggestions. I am also grateful to Marilyn Grobschmidt and Shena Redmond of Lynne Rienner Publishers for supervising the production of the book. Finally, I thank my wife, Parizad Tahbazzadeh, for her understanding while I wrote this book during weekends and holidays.

USAID has provided me challenging opportunities to explore democracy assistance. However, the views and opinions expressed here—as in my earlier books—are my own and do not necessarily reflect USAID policies and programs.

—*Krishna Kumar*

Promoting
Independent
Media

1

International Media Assistance

*A popular government without popular information or means of
acquiring it is but a prologue to a Farce or a Tragedy; or perhaps
both. Knowledge for ever will govern ignorance; and a people who
mean to be their own governors must arm themselves with the
power which knowledge gives.*

—James Madison

This book examines a relatively new phenomenon in international
development: assistance designed to promote robust, independent
media in developing and transitional societies. Such assistance is
based on an underlying assumption that independent media contributes to the building of democracy and economic development.

In the past, development efforts viewed the media as a tool for
achieving specific goals in agriculture, health, business, or education.
Now media assistance projects focus on the structure and journalistic
practice of the media itself. Such assistance seeks to lay the foundation for the emergence and consolidation of a media sector free of
state editorial or financial control, relying on advertising and sales
for its survival and growth. Media development efforts strive to
achieve the ideal of a "Fourth Estate," in which the press serves as a
complement and balance to the three branches of power—legislative,
executive, and judicial. The Fourth Estate, by virtue of its financial
and editorial independence, is supposed to hold state authorities
accountable by documenting the government's actions and nurture
democracy by encouraging an open but respectful exchange of ideas
and opinions.

The international community began providing media assistance starting in the late 1980s. Although precise data are unavailable, multilateral and bilateral donor agencies, private foundations, and international civil society organizations have since spent between $600 million and $1 billion on media projects.[1] Most of the assistance has gone to the Balkans, Eastern Europe, and Eurasia. However, Central America and Southern Africa have also received a modest share. There is now a perceptible shift of focus from the former communist bloc in Eastern and Southeastern Europe to other regions in Asia, Africa, and the Middle East that offer fresh challenges.

The substantive focus of media assistance programs has varied depending on the targeted country, the timing, and the donor. The majority of international media projects in the past focused on short-term and long-term training of journalists to improve professional standards and editorial content. Such training projects included consultant visits and publications of books on journalism. Donor governments have provided programmatic support to local media outlets to improve the quality of their news coverage and to increase audience share. Based on the assumption that commercial success is a necessary ingredient in forging independence from government or other vested interests, training initiatives have also imparted management and business skills to media managers.

Other programs have supported organizations, educational institutions, and media associations that promote media freedom and lobby for appropriate legislation and journalists' rights. In addition, donors have given direct financial and technical assistance to struggling media outlets in sensitive political conditions. Finally, European donors have tried to assist state-owned media enterprises in transforming them into genuine public service broadcasters in the tradition of European broadcasters.

Media Assistance and Public Diplomacy

Media development assistance is often confused with public-diplomacy media programs. Such confusion, though understandable, can be misleading. There is an important difference in their overall objectives as well as the strategies employed to achieve them.

Public diplomacy seeks to promote a country's foreign policy interests by informing and influencing the foreign audience. It is an instrument used to generate positive attitudes abroad toward a government's policies, programs, and social and political institutions. It complements traditional diplomacy because its primary focus is on nongovernmental actors. However, the objective of media assistance is to develop and strengthen the indigenous capacity for a free and unfettered flow of news and information, bolstering democratic institutions and culture.

These different objectives usually require different strategies. Media development involves strengthening local journalism and management skills, reforming the legal and regulatory regimes, helping and nourishing civil society organizations that promote a free press, and building an institutional environment that is conducive to the free flow of information and ideas. Public diplomacy media strategies, in comparison, entail broadcasting in foreign languages, providing favorable news stories to foreign media, advertising in newspapers and electronic media, and organizing exchange visits by foreign journalists and media managers. This approach seeks to use the modern media, with its vast audience and influence, to achieve specific foreign policy objectives.

Two recent examples of public-policy initiatives may illuminate this difference. In the aftermath of the terrorist attacks against the United States in September 2001, the US State Department funded advertisements in Middle Eastern media portraying the religious freedom enjoyed by Muslim citizens in this country. The purpose of these advertisements was to dispel popular misunderstandings about the American way of life and to emphasize the multiethnic composition of US society. In another case, Voice of America recently launched a program in the Farsi language that provides news and music to an Iranian audience. Its purpose is to promote the cause of democracy among Iranians. By all accounts, the program has a popular following in Iran. Although these two examples represent an effective use of media to further public diplomacy, and could possibly pave the way for the eventual emergence of free media outlets in the region, these efforts cannot be construed as independent media development.

When media assistance is primarily used as a tool of public diplomacy, it can sometimes be self-defeating. Blurring the distinction between the two endeavors creates false expectations in donor countries and genuine apprehensions in recipient nations. US policymakers, for example, would expect and demand that media projects promote a better understanding of our policies abroad, and evaluate the success and failure of such projects accordingly. They would also expect the media outlets benefiting from assistance to behave like a friend and not a critic and would be naturally disappointed when this did not happen.[2]

In recipient countries, merging media assistance with public diplomacy plays into skeptical attitudes about donor intentions. Government officials, political leaders, opinion makers, and academics are likely to resist, if not reject, media assistance because they might view it as a foreign effort to buy influence and manipulate their media sector. Given media assistance's roots in public diplomacy—such as broadcasts from Radio Free Europe and Voice of America to Eastern Europe and Eurasia—genuine apprehensions about US (or other foreign states') intentions exist in many parts of the world. Such apprehensions were epitomized by a remark made by President Vladimir Putin, who while discussing media issues with Russian nongovernmental organizations (NGOs) indicated that the purpose of media assistance was to further the interests of Western powers. To prevent such misconceptions that may undermine the success of media assistance, it is crucial to treat media development as distinct from public diplomacy.

Though they are separate tasks, media development and public diplomacy programs can still complement and reinforce one other. Often programs to develop indigenous media help public diplomacy efforts, and many public diplomacy interventions serve to promote independent media. The growth of independent media outlets can create space for public diplomacy. The Serbian case study in this book provides an excellent example. Independent media outlets nurtured by the international community enabled Western states to communicate their message directly to the Serbian public. Moreover, there are plenty of examples of public diplomacy contributing to the evolution of independent media. The former United States Information Service (which is now merged with the State Department) used to provide travel grants to journalists in developing countries to visit the United States. Such programs not only improved journalists' understanding and appreciation of US democratic institutions but also exposed them to the norms and workings of a free press. On their return, many of these journalists worked to promote greater freedom in their own societies.[3]

Growing Interest in Media Assistance

Several factors have contributed to the growing interest in media assistance. First, when a wave of democratic reform swept Africa,

Asia, and Latin America in the late 1980s, the international donor community started developing innovative programs for democracy promotion.

Such programs attempted to promote the development of civil society, economic and political decentralization, free and fair elections, and the rule of law. While pursuing these programs, donors realized that an independent media was a crucial element in building a functioning democratic system. The success of democratization efforts often depended on a free and unfettered flow of information and ideas. Elections could not be free or fair if the media remained under the manipulative control of a ruling party or government ministry. Civil society organizations could not thrive in the political arena if their voices never reached the public. The rule of law could not be built if citizens were denied the freedom to read, speak, and write as they wished. As a result of this awareness, the international community began to explore media assistance as an element of democratization efforts. The first international media assistance programs in the 1980s were relatively modest and largely focused on Latin American countries.

A major impetus for media development came as a result of the collapse of the Soviet Union and its hegemony over East European and Central Asian nations. In most of these countries, the underground press had played an important role in undermining authoritarian regimes. These underground outlets helped to strip away the legitimacy of communist rule by exposing its corrupt and dictatorial methods, developing informal communication networks, and enabling dissenting intellectuals and political leaders to reach a larger audience. There was a universal yearning for freedom of expression in these countries, and dissident leaders, social activists, writers, and academics established their own media outlets that reflected their views and aspirations. In Russia itself, *perestroika* and *glasnost* had opened up unprecedented opportunities for the emergence of independent media, free from state censorship and institutionalized self-censorship.

Responding to the end of Soviet rule, Western countries, particularly the United States, launched new media initiatives to upgrade journalistic, technical, and management skills and to foster an institutional environment supportive of a free press. The former Soviet Union and its satellites served as laboratories wherein the international community and its local partners refined different media development strategies and programs. Contemporary thinking on media assistance owes much to these efforts and experiences.

Second, tragic events in Rwanda and the former Yugoslavia amply demonstrated to policymakers and the public that the media, controlled by the state or particular ethnic factions, could be a powerful force in instigating and directing violence. As the media help to define the nature and implications of latent or manifest conflict for decisionmakers and shapes public opinion, biased, intolerant, and inaccurate reporting of events can inflame public passions and fears. In contrast, balanced reporting can reduce political tensions and contribute to the resolution of conflict.

As a result, during the 1990s the international community started supporting a wide array of media projects in countries torn apart by civil wars. Donors focused on the postconflict phase, when war had subsided and some semblance of order had been established. Prime examples are Bosnia, Croatia, East Timor, Kosovo, and Serbia, each of which has received significant media assistance. The international community has also been funding modest initiatives in many African countries—such as Burundi, Congo, and Liberia—to ease ethnic and religious tensions while promoting tolerance and peaceful coexistence.

Third, the information revolution that is transforming the global economy has also contributed to an increased international involvement in the media. Such changes have underscored the potentially critical role played by the media in economic growth and transformation. A broad consensus has emerged among development experts that economic growth and media freedom are often intertwined. As former World Bank president James Wolfensohn put it, "To reduce poverty, we must liberate access to information and improve the quality of information. People with more information are empowered to make better choices" (World Bank Institute 2002, v). Farmers, businessworkers, traders, bankers, entrepreneurs, industrialists, monetary and fiscal experts, and the general citizenry require a free flow of information to make the best decisions. And the information in demand pertains not only to financial but also to social and political factors that shape the economic environment, creating opportunities and incentives for individual entrepreneurship.

Although the current approach to media assistance emerged in recent years, development experts dating back to the 1950s recognized the importance of the media and modern communications in fighting pervasive poverty. The theoretical justification for focusing on the media came from experts such as Daniel Lerner and Wilber Schram, who examined the complex process through which the media engenders economic and social change. Daniel Lerner's *Passing Away of Traditional Society: Modernizing the Middle East,* which analyzed the role of mass media in the Middle East's modernization process, has had a profound influence on development theory.

Fourth, there is a widespread recognition that independent media contributes to public accountability, curtailing widespread corruption that plagues economic and political institutions in the developing world. The experience of developed democracies shows that investigative journalism saves taxpayers' money and improves the performance of public institutions by driving out corrupt officials. Although the presence of independent media is no panacea for effective government, it does help in creating responsive political culture and public institutions.

Finally, the threat of terrorism has also stimulated policymakers' interest in independent media development. For example, many foreign-policy experts suggest that the absence of democracy in the Middle East, particularly in countries deemed to be Western allies, has directly and indirectly contributed to the growth of international terrorism. Because these countries do not permit internal dissent and debate, public anger and frustration against the government is often directed toward the West, particularly the United States. A significant portion of the public blames the United States and other Western countries for their government's failures. To address this phenomenon, democratic institutions—including a free press—need to be promoted and nurtured in these countries to enable opposition parties and voices to participate in the political process. US foreign policy makers now place a priority on independent media development in the Middle East. Many initiatives are under way.

All of these factors—a wave of democratic reform, the collapse of Soviet rule, media-fueled sectarian war, the information revolution, the threat of terrorism, and concerns about corrupt governance—have contributed to the growing engagement of the international donor community in media development. Despite their enthusiasm for media assistance, donors tend to have realistic expectations about what independent media can or cannot achieve. They are acutely aware that in many societies emerging from totalitarian or autocratic rule, the media's role is compromised by tainted economic, social, and political structures that undermine economic growth and political freedom.

Actors in International Media Assistance

Since the early 1990s the number of international actors engaged in media assistance has increased dramatically, reflecting enhanced public and policy interest and funding. These actors fall generally into two categories—donors and intermediaries. Donors provide resources whereas intermediary organizations design and implement projects, usually in cooperation with local partners in the recipient countries.[4]

Three kinds of international donors—bilateral donor agencies, international governmental organizations, and private foundations— deserve particular mention. Bilateral agencies continue to be the major source of funding for media development. Among them, the United States Agency for International Development (USAID) has been the largest donor, providing more than $260 million in media assistance over the past decade. Most of its assistance has gone to the Balkans, Eastern and Central Europe, and Eurasia. Other prominent bilateral agency donors include the Canadian International Development Agency (CIDA), the British Department for International Development (DFID), and the Swedish International Development Agency.

A number of intergovernmental organizations also provide support for media development. These include the United Nations, the World Bank, the European Commission (EC), the Council of Europe, the Organization for Security and Cooperation in Europe (OSCE), and the United Nations Educational, Scientific, and Cultural Organization (UNESCO). The largest donor in this subcategory is the European Commission, which has worked in partnership with other international organizations such as the OSCE, European Reconstruction Agency (EAR), and Council of Europe. In addition, it has also directly funded media outlets, NGOs, and educational institutions, and in some cases EC funding has exceeded USAID levels. The World Bank is also becoming more active in the media sector and may emerge in the future as a major actor because of its financial and intellectual clout.

Many large and small private foundations have also supported the growth of media in developing and transition countries. These include the Ford Foundation, the Independent Journalism Foundation, the John S. and James L. Knight Foundation, the MacArthur Foundation, the Markle Foundation, the Rockefeller Foundation, and the Soros Foundation Network. Three German foundations—Friedrich Ebert, Friedrich Naumann, and Konrad Adenauer Stitungen—have also funded media projects. Most of these foundations have given grants for short- and long-term journalism training, exchange visits for journalists, and international dialogues and meetings. However, the Soros Foundation Network, including the Open Society Institute, has played an influential role in many postcommunist countries in Europe and Eurasia and has funded a wide variety of media interventions.

Most donors work with intermediary organizations as they lack technical expertise and organizational resources to design and implement media programs. In the case of major bilateral agencies, such as USAID, this course is politically prudent as well. Often the recipient countries are more receptive if media assistance is provided through established intermediary organizations rather than from the bilateral donor directly.

Two NGOs have received the lion's share of US government media assistance funding, Internews and the International Research and Exchanges Board (IREX). Internews has also received funds from many European donors, including the European Commission and the UK's DFID, as well as national and international foundations. IREX has been active largely in Eastern Europe and Eurasia. Like Internews, it has been providing multifaceted media assistance, ranging from training to legal assistance and strengthening local media organizations. IREX has tended to work more with print media than Internews, though programs vary from country to country. There is also a slight difference in overall strategy, with Internews establishing its own affiliate in a country whereas IREX works with existing indigenous institutions and media outlets.

Several European media NGOs have gained a reputation for experience and excellence in media assistance. Amsterdam-based Press Now receives funds from the Dutch government as well as other donors. It has worked extensively on myriad projects in the Balkans and Eastern Europe, providing training, equipment, and managerial advice. Other important NGOs include the Danish Baltic Media Center (funded mainly by the Danish government), Medienhilfe in Switzlerland, and London-based Article 19, which seeks to promote media freedom through legal advice and advocacy.

In addition, there are many media organizations that seek to defend the rights of journalists and news organizations, fight censorship, and offer educational and training programs. Paris-based Rapporteur sans Frontières publicizes and protests abuses of media freedom around the world. The International Federation of Journalists in Brussels is a membership organization of journalists' associations from different countries. Similarly, the World Association of Newspapers provides a global platform for publishers, and the International Press Institute links editors, publishers, journalists, and academics (Darbishire 2002, 332).

Many universities have established media centers and received funds from donors to undertake training and educational programs. For example, as described in Chapter 3, Florida International University has received funds from USAID to manage a large journalism training program in Central America. Finally, commercial consulting firms have also entered the arena of media assistance. Several US firms have designed, managed, and implemented media assistance projects; among them are Creative Associates, Development Alternatives, and Management Systems International.

Origin of the Book

Despite substantial international investment in media assistance, little has been written about the field. There are no books, doctoral theses, or even research articles in professional journals analyzing the subject and the possible effect of media aid. Although there is a growing literature on emerging media in developing and transitional countries, such literature does not examine the role of international assistance. At best there are only superficial references to existing or planned international efforts.

The lack of literature on international media assistance is not so surprising. Large-scale assistance for building independent media is relatively new, having begun in the 1990s. Much of the information about these programs remains embedded in the experiences of the practitioners still heavily engaged in developing projects. Unfortunately, these practitioners have had little time to systematically reflect on their experiences and record them for others. Moreover, many international donors engaged in media assistance have preferred to take a low profile because of the political sensitivities involved.

This book represents one step in explaining international efforts to promote independent media. It attempts to examine the nature and significance of media assistance, discussing the evolution of the field, the focus of various programming approaches, and the possible impact of such efforts. It presents case studies of media assistance programs in different countries.The book concludes with a set of recommendations for expanding and deepening media assistance for the international community.

This book project grew out of a multi-country study that I directed in 2002–2004 to examine media assistance programs funded by the US Agency for International Development. The overall purpose of the study was to assess the nature and effectiveness of USAID programs and make policy and programmatic recommendations for the future. In writing this book I have mostly drawn from the massive information collected during two years of research and analysis.

The book is based primarily on three sources of information. First are reviews of literature covering scholarly writings, project and program documents, and articles in popular magazines and newspapers on media assistance. Such reviews were country specific as well as global in nature. Because the academic literature is extremely limited and media assistance is hardly covered in magazines and newspapers except in high-profile cases such as Bosnia and Serbia, reviews largely relied on program documentation. I had the unique advantage of perusing thousands of documents that are not available to the public. Although mostly descriptive and often self-serving, they identified critical gaps in our knowledge and illuminated the challenges and achievements of international media endeavors.

Second, my colleagues and I undertook extensive fieldwork in seven countries/regions—Afghanistan, Bosnia, Central America, Indonesia, Russia, Serbia, and Sierra Leone. In each of these cases, research teams conducted extensive discussions with international donor agencies, officials of host countries, project staff and contractors, and local media experts and journalists. Every possible effort was made to interview all those experts and managers who had intimate knowledge of the ongoing media assistance programs. Teams also examined locally available documents and reports and used translators to translate documents into English when necessary. In the absence of hard quantitative data, they largely relied on available documentation, in-depth interviews, and their own knowledge of the media scene for their findings and conclusions.

Finally, I organized a series of meetings in Washington, D.C., to discuss the findings of the country studies and explore new directions for media assistance programs. Such meetings helped to identify many problems and challenges facing media assistance programs and helped in formulating a set of recommendation for policymakers.

Two criteria have been used in selecting countries for this book. Every effort has been made to include at least one country from Asia, Africa, Latin America, and Europe. Second, and more important, every effort has been made to include countries that were major recipients of international media assistance.

Organization of the Book

In addition to this introductory chapter, the book contains nine others. Chapter 2 explains the major programming approaches that the international community has used to promote the growth of independent media. These approaches include improving journalistic skills and expertise, promoting the economic viability of independent media enterprises, reforming existing legal and regulatory regimes, strengthening media organizations, promoting the transformation of state media outlets, and building alternative media. All these approaches are mutually complementary and reinforcing. International donors have employed each of these strategies at some point, taking into consideration the local conditions and circumstances.

Chapter 3 focuses on the Latin American Journalism Project (LAJP), which was the first major international initiative to promote independent media. Managed by Florida International University and funded by the US Agency for International Development, the project trained thousands of journalists in Central America, established a regional journalism training center in Panama, and left a lasting impression on the media scene in the region. This chapter describes the structure of the project, its achievements and limitations, and the factors that affected its performance and efficacy. It also identifies a set of lessons to be drawn from the project.

Chapter 4 describes a major media assistance project designed to promote the growth of independent, regional television stations in the Russian Federation. This project, called the Independent Television Project, was launched by Internews in 1992 with financial support from USAID. The project has contributed to the emergence of about 600 regional television stations that are economically viable. The chapter describes the conditions under which the project was launched and the factors that have contributed to its success.

Chapter 5 looks at Serbia, where independent media, with generous international assistance, played an important role in the defeat of Slobodan Milosevic in the 2000 elections. The chapter explains the nature of international assistance and how it helped alternative media outlets in the country survive Milosevic's authoritarian rule and eventually overthrow it. The chapter also discusses the special media assistance programs that were devised for the elections, and it explains post-Milosevic developments in international assistance.

Chapter 6 recounts an ambitious but flawed attempt by US and European donors to establish a multiethnic, tolerant broadcasting network in Bosnia-Herzegovina after the signing of the Dayton peace agreement. Known as the Open Broadcasting Network, the project was meant to provide an alternative to ultranationalist broadcasters by offering balanced coverage of news and events without ethnic or religious prejudice. The chapter examines how the project was launched, its conflicting goals, its achievements and setbacks, and the lessons it holds for future media efforts in similar settings.

Chapter 7 focuses on a project assisting fifty independent radio stations in Indonesia. The project, launched after the fall of President Suharto's regime, provided journalism training, equipment, technical assistance, and programming support to participating radio stations. The chapter examines the impact of the assistance on the radio stations and the radio sector as a whole.

Chapter 8 discusses international media assistance to Afghanistan after the collapse of the Taliban regime in 2001. It particularly examines a major project that seeks to establish a network of community radio stations throughout the country to broadcast local and national news and public affairs programs. It discusses the nature of international assistance, the working of newly established radio stations, and the challenges they face. The chapter also examines the prospects for their survival after international assistance dries up.

The subsequent chapter describes Talking Drum Studio in Sierra Leone, which seeks to promote peace and reconciliation in that war-torn society. Funded by multiple donors and managed by Search for Common Ground, the studio produces entertaining but educational radio programs—news features, stories, dramas, and even sport events—that are distributed to participating radio stations. These programs have been quite popular with a cross-section of the people. The chapter discusses the nature and working of the studio and its overall impact on improving the climate for peace.

Chapter 10 rounds out the book by outlining recommendations for future media assistance efforts.

Clarifying the Terms

A few expressions in this book are used to communicate the main ideas and case studies but require clarification to avoid confusion. *The media* is broadly defined to encompass both print and broadcast media. It includes newspapers, periodicals, magazines, radio and television stations, and even the Internet. It does not refer to telephone communications. As conceptualized here, *media assistance* refers to economic, technical, and financial assistance provided by the international community to build and strengthen independent media. Its primary purpose is to develop an indigenous media sector that promotes democracy and development. *Independent media* indicates nonstate media or media enterprises owned by individuals, corporations, and nonprofit organizations. Such a definition sets aside separate considerations about the possible control over media by vested economic and political interests.[5] An underlying premise and objective of media assistance is to uphold journalistic inquiry and to support news organizations that are editorially independent and free of direct political control.

The international community refers to all bilateral and multilateral donor agencies, international organizations and associations, international NGOs, private foundations, and other organized groups engaged in international assistance. This term obviously does not imply that all these international agencies and groups speak with one voice or share identical objectives.

War-torn societies indicates those countries with ongoing low- and high-intensity conflicts, whereas *postconflict societies* refers to the countries in which peace accords have been signed or one party of the conflict has emerged victorious. Postconflict societies can face renewed tensions and violence, thereby acquiring the status of war-torn societies. *Transitional societies* is used to describe a relative level of social and economic development in which a totalitarian or autocratic political order has collapsed, opening the way for liberalization and democratization.

Notes

1. No precise figures are available. This estimate is from Hume 2002, p. 3.

2. A USAID official once bitterly complained to me about a Serbian newspaper that had received US assistance but had criticized US policies in the country. The official was disappointed because he saw the purpose of assistance as a way of winning friends for the United States, not developing indigenous media.

3. I met many journalists in Africa who after their sojourn to Europe and the United States waged a struggle for press freedom in their own societies.

4. For an excellent discussion of the various actors involved in international media assistance programs, please see Price, Noll, and De Luce 2002. This document was contracted by USAID to the Program in Comparative Media Law and Policy, Center for Socio-Legal Studies, at Oxford University.

5. I am fully aware of the limitations of the term. I have followed this definition for empirical rather than conceptual reasons. In many developing and transitional countries, there is often no way to find out who controls a media outlet. Moreover, the loyalties of media owners change over time.

2

Programming Approaches to Independent Media Building

To preserve the freedom of the human mind then and the freedom of the press, every spirit should be ready to devote itself to martyrdom.
—Thomas Jefferson

How does the international community promote independent media? This chapter seeks to answer that question by explaining the major programming approaches that the donor community has pursued in its media development efforts. Particular attention is devoted to programming approaches that are mutually reinforcing and have been widely employed.

These programming approaches have evolved over time, as the United States and other donors have grappled with the challenge of strengthening independent media in different social and political systems. For example, earlier media programs largely focused on improving journalistic skills and expertise. But working in Eastern Europe and countries in the former Soviet Union, the international community realized that journalism training was not sufficient to engender an independent media space, as the survival of newly founded or privatized media outlets largely depended upon their management and business capabilities. Therefore, international organizations also started fashioning interventions on the business side of the media. While working in the newly freed countries in Europe and Eurasia, the international community also became aware of the importance of legal and regulatory regimes and started developing programs that provided training and technical assistance for legal and regulatory reform. Furthermore, it started focusing on promoting and strengthening a set of organizations—journalist associations, trade organizations, advertising agencies, polling firms, and educational institutions—that are essential to create and sustain an enabling environment for the media. Thus there has been a steady learning curve for donors, which has broadened the nature and focus of media intervention strategies.

This chapter presents six programming approaches that have supported media intervention in transitional and postconflict societies. They are, in order, journalism training and education, promoting economic viability, financial and commodity assistance, legal and regulatory reform, building institutional infrastructure, and transformation of state-owned media enterprises.

Improving Journalistic Skills and Expertise

The most common programming approach has been to help improve the professional skills of both print and broadcast media journalists. Given that developing and transitional countries lacked and still lack adequate training facilities for journalists, the importance of this strategy cannot be overemphasized. Most major donors have supported training initiatives for journalists and are likely to continue to do so in the near future.

Short-term training is generally provided to working journalists within the country. Such training, which ranges from two to five days in duration, tends to be practical, helping journalists learn skills that can be readily applied. Short-term training programs focus on topics such as writing, reporting, and editing news stories; investigative reporting; and the existing laws and regulations governing media. Short-term training also has been used to expose local journalists to methods of news reporting and coverage, emphasizing practices such as multiple checking of sources and presentation of different viewpoints. Some short-term training includes courses on professional ethics, editorial independence, and the characteristics of a free press. In addition, short-term training may prepare journalists to cover special events and issues such as elections, ethnic conflicts, humanitarian assistance, and environmental degradation. Medium-term training programs, which tend to run from one to eight weeks, cover similar subjects and skills.

Short-term training has proved quite popular for many reasons. Media owners and managers prefer it, as it often produces demonstrable improvements within a limited time frame. Moreover, it does not take employees away for a long time. Many media outlets in transitional and war-torn societies have minimal staff and therefore cannot spare journalists for training for more than a few days. Trainees are also happy because it improves their skills and expertise relatively quickly. Given the low cost of short-term training, a large number of journalists can be trained within a project, partly explaining the fascination of international donors and media NGOs with this approach. Donors are attracted to short-term training because it involves less risk or controversy and minimal project management from a donor, as it does not attempt to transform a particular news organization or tackle systemic problems within a media sector.

In addition to short- and medium-term training, international agencies sometimes provide overseas long-term training, ranging from six to twelve months, to promising journalists. Such training takes many forms, from formal enrollment in journalism educational institutions for a degree program to apprenticeship in media outlets, wherein the journalists acquire field experience. The advantage of long-term training in a journalism institution is that it provides a systematic and comprehensive exposure for trainees both in the theory and practice of journalism (Kumar 2004, 6). The problem is that such training tends to be expensive. For example, the cost of long-term training in the United States per student in an educational institution ranges from $80,000 to $120,000.[1] Compared to short-term training, only a small number of journalists can be trained with the same resources.

Apprenticeships in Western media outlets are undoubtedly less expensive than professional training at universities, as no tuition fees are required. Moreover, such training is practical, and the trainees get exposed to a wide range of routine tasks and activities. I have met many Asian journalists who had the opportunity to work at US newspapers and found the experience rewarding. Many small foundations have promoted apprenticeships and have awarded scholarships to deserving candidates. It usually takes time and effort to find suitable media firms that are willing to take foreign apprentices, however.

During the early 1990s, foreign staff conducted much of the journalism training in the Balkans, Eastern Europe, and Russia. This was unavoidable because local experts lacked experience working in a free media environment. The use of foreign trainers created some problems. Because they lacked knowledge of local languages and of the environment in which the journalists worked, their training was not always productive. They often cited examples from their own experiences in Western democracies that made little sense to the participants in their courses.[2] Foreign trainers had greater success when they focused on technical topics such as camera operation, film editing, design and layout, or news management.

During the past decade, a cadre of local trainers has emerged in many countries that are increasingly called upon by the international community. Such trainers either are the product of Western journalism institutions or have participated in international donor assistance programs and as a result have acquired necessary skills and expertise. International donors also organize intensive courses for the selected candidates, who in turn train new trainees. The caliber of such trainers has been constantly improving, and most of the international NGOs now have a list of indigenous trainers from the same country or region. The emergence of local trainers has resulted in two positive developments, which in turn have promoted the growth of professional journalism skills. First, because it costs less to hire a local trainer than to bring in experts from the United States or Europe, more aspiring journalists have been trained within the same budget. Second, as the local trainers invariably possess a better understanding of the conditions in which journalists work than do foreign trainers, the training often has proved more relevant to the needs of the journalists and the media owners (Kumar 2004, 5).

Comprehensive training programs tend to generate multiplier effects.[3] Often, the journalists who receive training share their newly acquired expertise with their colleagues. This happens without any conscious design or effort. Junior colleagues often learn by watching or assisting the trained professionals, particularly in the case of broadcast media. For example, in regional television stations in Russia, many fellow journalists learned techniques of editing or reporting a story simply by assisting their trained colleagues. In other cases, the presence and example of trained professionals encouraged others to improve their skills.

Sometimes international media organizations work with local educational training institutions to conduct training, to reach more aspiring journalists and leave behind a "legacy" after a project has expired. They provide grants and technical assistance to these institutions to improve their curricula, upgrade their technical capabilities, and even retrain their teachers. Examples include the Montenegro Media Institute, the Albania Media Institute, the Slovak Media Institute, and the City TV Foundation in Slovakia, all of which have been funded by USAID. Such assistance helps to build local institutional training capacity. In addition, many donors have given grants to local journalism institutions to upgrade teaching and research capabilities. One promising approach is to link a journalism training institute/university with a counterpart in the United States or some other developed democracy.

As a part of training and educational efforts, international media NGOs also publish books, monographs, and manuals in local languages on different aspects of journalism. These are either translated from English textbooks or written in local languages. Because of the widespread shortage of suitable material, such publications can be extremely useful and tend to be in high demand. For example, as Chapter 7 notes, some publications are even out of print in Indonesia because of their popularity. In Latin America, the publication of journalism books in Spanish generated revenues for a training institute.

Promoting Economic Viability of Media Enterprises

The second of the six approaches is based on the simple yet often-overlooked principle that the economic viability of media enterprises is a necessary, though not a sufficient, condition for the growth of independent and responsible media. Prospects for a successful media firm depend on sound business management as well as sales and advertising that at minimum cover operating costs and expenses. Moreover, profitable, privately owned media firms tend to be less vulnerable to editorial control and manipulation because they are not dependent on subsidies and favors from vested state or business interests.

The donor community promotes economic viability in numerous ways. It supports the training of media managers and directors of advertising and public relations. Such projects include general and specialized training. The general courses focus on senior executives and managers who are taught basic aspects of business operations; specialized instruction is designed for junior and middle-level managers. Often the courses are short-term, ranging from a day to a few days, providing trainees with a general exposure to a specific field. In the past, most of the business development programs, especially in Central Europe and Eurasia, focused on specialized training for middle-level media executives. As middle-level managers in these countries had little or no experience in running businesses, and because educational opportunities for business education were limited, the training achieved positive results. The courses exposed trainees to the challenges of running a commercial media operation and imparted skills for supervising technical and professional staff.

International organizations also arrange for in-house consultancies. Under such arrangements, outside experts visit a media outlet and actually help in improving its management and business practices. They also assist in solving specific problems facing media outlets. For example, if a newspaper is having trouble soliciting advertisers, the consultant may look into the matter and suggest some practical steps. If there is high turnover among reporters, consultants can examine the reasons and advise management accordingly. In-house consultancies have proven effective in Eastern Europe and Russia. However, it is necessary that consultants are experienced managers, having in-country experience. The challenge is finding and recruiting such consultants. For example, international NGOs working in former socialist countries in Europe found it extremely difficult to recruit qualified consultants. Often the outside consultants failed to fully understand the intricacies of patron-client relationships in the economic climate of these postcommunist countries. Consequently, the consultants' recommendations were not always practical.

In addition, international organizations also try to promote a level playing field for independent and state media enterprises. Such efforts are important because state-owned media enterprises usually enjoy many advantages over their commercial counterparts. Often state media pay little or no rent, enjoy tax advantages, and receive preferential treatment in access to news and information. Working with local NGOs and experts, the international community in some cases has lobbied governments into taking legal and administrative steps to ensure that all media outlets operate under the same rules and regulations and receive fair treatment. For example, such lobbying may insist that commercial media enterprises pay the same tax rates that state media pay or receive the same exemptions from taxes and excise duties that state media enjoy. In countries where state television dominates the airwaves, the international community has even demanded restrictions on the share of total advertisement sales or airtime on state television in order to allow nonstate media a fair share of the advertising market.

The economic viability of a media company is closely related to existing economic conditions. Unless a country has a growing private sector, an independent media sector cannot flourish. For example, in sub-Saharan countries, the organized private sector is not only small but is also dependent on the patronage of the government. In such countries, commercial and industrial firms could be penalized if they advertise in newspapers or other media outlets that are critical of the government. As a result, in spite of constitutional guarantees for media freedom, independent media hardly exist in these societies. The independent media outlets that do operate remain in an extremely precarious situation. Transitional and war-torn societies also lack the economic, legal, and political institutions and conditions that promote the growth of a vibrant private sector—and this remains a major bottleneck to the growth, survival, and sustainability of independent media outlets in these countries.

Sustaining Independent Media Through Financial and Commodity Assistance

Sometimes international actors also help establish new or sustain existing media outlets through financial assistance or donations of equipment. Such assistance is usually given to selected media outlets that display journalistic excellence and play a role in democratization and peace building.

International donors have given financial assistance to the media mostly in war-torn societies, where media enterprises were literally bankrupt and could not manage without outside assistance. For example, in Bosnia-Herzegovina, USAID and many other international donors gave financial assistance to newspapers, magazines, and radio stations that were in dire need of resources. Though the aid started on a modest scale in early 1995, such assistance rapidly expanded after the signing of the Dayton peace agreement in November of that year. International NGOs have financially helped independent media outlets in Afghanistan, East Timor, Kosovo, and Serbia as well. In Liberia, USAID funded Star Radio, an independent station, which the government later closed. In the past, community radio stations operating in small rural communities have received both financial and commodity assistance from international donors, particularly in Latin America. The assistance is channeled through NGOs, and even the state agencies, because the volume of assistance tends to be small.

Much of the assistance is given in kind. For example, international donors provided newsprint and in some cases printing presses to selected newspapers and periodicals in the Balkans. They donated cameras, video editing equipment, computers, and even transmitters and receivers to selected radio and television stations. The contribution of equipment was accompanied by technical assistance and training to teach recipients how to effectively use the technology. Some donors prefer such assistance because the chances of misusing equipment are undoubtedly less than direct financial assistance.

The weight of expert opinion discourages direct injections of money for media outlets. Such assistance breeds a culture of dependency among recipients. Outlets often become accustomed to outside help and resist taking painful but necessary measures, such as cutting costs, reducing staff, and seeking additional advertising revenues. The experience of Open Broadcast Network, discussed in Chapter 6, illustrates this point. The experience of many war-torn societies, particularly Bosnia-Herzegovina, indicates that the high proportion of media outlets launched with foreign assistance did not survive once the assistance ceased because the outlets found it difficult to submit themselves to market discipline. However, many indigenous efforts that received minimal outside assistance survived, primarily because they operated with shoestring budgets. Moreover, there is always a question of favoritism. Media outlets singled out for help arouse suspicion and envy among others. They are even looked at as foreign mouthpieces. Transparent procedures to award assistance are essential when financial assistance is given. Large sums of cash donated without strict conditions can be misused by managers and owners. Instead of strengthening struggling media outlets, these funds might enrich their owners. There have been, for example, many complaints about the misuse of direct assistance in former Yugoslavia.

However, direct financial assistance cannot be totally ruled out in many transitional or war-torn countries, in which outside assistance is absolutely necessary to revive existing print and broadcast media outlets or to establish new ones. Struggling media enterprises urgently need money in countries such as Afghanistan, East Timor, and Iraq.

Promoting Legal and Regulatory Reforms

Since the beginning of media assistance, experts and policymakers have recognized that sound legal and regulatory regimes are essential to the flowering of independent media. Absent supporting legal systems and appropriate regulatory mechanisms, no amount of journalism training or business acumen can make much of an impact on the media landscape.

At least two categories of laws support the media's ability to function effectively (Price and Krug 2002). The first category includes legislation concerning the ownership and control of media. Existing laws should not only permit private ownership but also ensure that private media is not discriminated against by government-owned media enterprises. Therefore, registration procedures, licensing of print and broadcast media, and access to information are critically important. The second category relates to laws pertaining to freedom of the press (direct or indirect censorship), libel, privacy, and sedition. Journalists must be free to report and analyze, and what is forbidden should be strictly and narrowly defined. When the definitions are imprecise, the authorities can use such ambiguity to silence journalists. Libel laws should safeguard media freedom, as the threat of libel can deter inquisitive journalists from undertaking investigative journalism. Ideally, a media outlet should be free to report what it considers, in good faith, to be true. The burden of the proof should be on the plaintiff, not on the journalist.

The international community seeks to foster an enabling legal and regulatory environment through technical assistance to concerned governmental and nongovernmental organizations. For example, in Central and Eastern European countries, international media organizations supported independent analyses of laws pertaining to the press, which proved to be valuable in educating concerned policy- and decision-makers in the government and the public. Donors and NGOs also gave technical assistance to both the executive and legislative government branches for drafting appropriate media laws and regulations. Media NGOs organized training and technical assistance programs for regulatory bodies, legislative bodies, and executive branches. They developed legal seminars and materials covering many areas, such as broadcasting laws, press laws, laws to protect journalists, and defamation and libel laws. Such projects help with the drafting of new laws or revising existing ones and provide standards against which the new legislation is judged. Similar assistance also has been provided to countries such as Cambodia, El Salvador, Ethiopia, Nicaragua, and Uganda during the early phase of democratic transition.

In addition, the international community supports indigenous media and civil society organizations that seek to exert public pressure on the government for necessary reforms. The underlying rationale is that legal and regulatory reforms in a transitional or postconflict society cannot be initiated and sustained without indigenous support—journalists, media entities, and the civil society organizations. Many donor agencies, such as USAID, have provided generous assistance to indigenous civil society organizations who give technical assistance to the various branches of the government and educate and mobilize public opinion for legal reforms. In countries such as Bosnia, Guatemala, Russia, and Serbia, indigenous civil society organizations played an active role in pushing for reforms as well as in safeguarding the progress already made.

Many transitional and war-torn countries suffer from an acute shortage of well-trained lawyers who specialize in media law. Media lawyers are needed to assist individual media enterprises, help journalists being persecuted by government or other interests, and to assist independent regulatory bodies. International agencies have funded training programs and even the establishment of special media courses in existing law faculties in local universities. The Moscow Media Law and Policy Center (recently renamed the Institute for Information Laws) provides a good example. Initially funded by a number of international donors, the institute has emerged as a respected training and consulting organization, playing an important role in Russia and neighboring countries (Kumar and Cooper 2003). USAID has also supported the establishment of a similar institute, the Media Law and Policy Center in Indonesia, which despite some initial teething troubles is emerging as an important actor on the Indonesian media scene (Kalathil and Kumar 2005).

The national and international advocates for legal and regulatory reform face many obstacles. Governments are usually reluctant to introduce major legal reforms that would undermine their direct and indirect control over the media. The legislative process to revise or draft new media legislation is usually time-consuming and requires political will and commitment that are usually absent. In the case of the broadcast media, many firms that own broadcasting licenses oppose an open system because that would challenge their dominant position. This was the case in Serbia, for example, where many of the pro-Milosevic broadcasting stations opposed broadcasting reforms. Progress in changing criminal libel laws in most countries tends to be slow because of the opposition of government officials and political leaders.

Consequently, the pace of legal and regulatory reforms tends to be slow and halting. For example, Albania took seven years after the fall of the dictatorial regime to pass and implement new media laws. After four years of a new government, Slovakia has only half of the media laws that are deemed necessary for a free press. In the Balkans, Bosnia is the only country that has successfully instituted essential legal reforms and constituted a relatively independent regulatory board. Its Communications Regulatory Agency has established transparent, fair broadcast regulation that removed political manipulation from the licensing process and has virtually eliminated inflammatory broad-casts (De Luce 2003).[4] Even when new media laws were passed, they did not meet the standards of Western laws. For example, in Serbia, the new government successfully pushed a new broadcasting law through the legislature, but the enacted law was considered flawed by many legal experts. Sometimes, sections of newly enacted media laws were amenable to different interpretations or were contradictory, as has been the case in Russia.

Proper implementation of the enacted laws is always a problem (Kumar 2004). To maintain a grip on the media, ruling political parties and government officials find loopholes in legislation that violate the spirit of the law. They also manipulate the newly reconstituted or established regulatory agencies that fail to frame and follow transparent procedures for establishing and registering new media enterprises and regulate the established ones. In most transitional and war-torn countries, the judiciary is weak and susceptible to political pressures. Widespread corruption in law enforcement agencies also impedes implementation of new legislation. Aggrieved journalists and media owners find it more prudent to remain silent than to wage long, expensive legal battles with little prospect for success. Ignorance of the newly enacted press laws often is widespread, and journalists are not aware of their legal rights and responsibilities. The paucity of the lawyers proficient in media law and its application compounds the problem.

Strengthening Institutional Infrastructure for Media

The international community also helps in building and strengthening institutional infrastructure for independent media. Donors have supported a whole set of organizations, such as journalism institutions, journalists' associations, trade associations, advertising agencies, audience research and polling organizations, and prodemocracy civil society organizations, which help nurture a vibrant independent media sector.

Some international donors have given assistance to existing journalism departments in universities or supported the establishment of new journalism training centers. Assistance to universities aims to improve educational curriculum, improve technical capacities, and enhance the expertise of the faculty. Experience has shown that such assistance does not produce immediate results. Amending a curriculum can be a time-consuming and tedious process. Older faculty members sometimes resist new ideas or changes to the curriculum. In many transitional countries, the faculty are mainly social scientists and lack direct journalism experience. As a result, they remain more comfortable in teaching theory than the craft of journalism. However, it is important that the international community continue to focus on teaching and research institutions. Only established educational institutions can provide long-term training to journalists and cultivate the next generation of journalism teachers and researchers.

The international community also assists journalists' associations, as they can help protect reporters, institutionalize professional norms and ethics, and advance the journalism profession. Donors have provided grants to hold professional meetings, publish journalism directories, and organize training programs to improve journalism standards. Assistance has also focused on encouraging regional networks, as has been the case in Central America, Southeast Asia, and Central Europe. These professional networks hold regional gatherings, give awards for outstanding journalism, and sometimes seek to protect journalists from persecution by governments. As most governments are sensitive to international press, such professional organizations help to promote a free media.

The fragmentation of the journalistic community has sometimes presented a problem for international donors. Multiple journalists' organizations often exist even in small countries, which compete for membership and resources. For example, broadcasters were at one point represented by five different associations in Bosnia (IREX 2002, 8). Different political parties may also promote certain associations that are friendly to them, as has been the case in Cambodia. The presence of multiple journalists' associations in a country naturally undermines their effectiveness and reduces their bargaining power. Donors can do little to promote a single journalists' association except exert subtle pressure on those organizations that receive its assistance to unite.[5]

As with journalists, donors also encourage media owners to form their own trade associations to articulate their interests. Donors have given technical assistance to new media associations to draft rules and regulations in transitional countries and, in some cases, have even subsidized recurring expenses for an initial period. In addition, donors have funded foreign trips for the leaders and staff of these organizations so that they become acquainted with the working of similar organizations in developed democracies or in other transitional countries.

Internews and IREX have successfully promoted media trade organizations in many countries in Central and Eastern Europe and Eurasia.

Trade organizations focus more on economic and political problems their members face than on the challenges to press freedom posed by government or other vested interests. Like journalists' associations, they often remain fragmented in many countries. Owners of media firms often see each other as competitors rather than partners and sometimes are reluctant to cooperate too closely. However, anecdotal evidence indicates that media trade organizations come together when they face a major crisis or threat.[6]

In Eastern and Central Europe and the Balkans, the international community has also helped to promote advertising and marketing agencies, polling and audience research firms, and private consulting agencies. Establishment of advertising firms was necessary to attract advertisements for newly established or newly privatized media enterprises. Polling and audience research firms were also needed to assess the market and, more important, to establish ratings for media outlets. Donors have provided technical and even commodity assistance to such firms while also providing funds to broadcast media outlets to pay for advertising or audience research services from the firms. In countries such as Bosnia, Serbia, Bulgaria, and Russia, marketing and audience research firms have taken on an increasingly important role. Media outlets now turn to these firms for their services to sell advertising and to improve programming. Marketing and poll research firms, often with the assistance of Western media firms, have started audience research surveys. However, the reliability of the surveys remains dubious in many cases, and a perception persists that the findings are sometimes compromised.[7]

Aid that falls in the category of civil-society assistance can also benefit efforts to build an independent media sector. Many prodemocracy groups—human rights organizations, think tanks, research organizations—that receive international assistance also support the idea of a free press.

In addition to building institutional infrastructure, the international community supports repairing and building physical communications infrastructure in war-torn societies. In Afghanistan, Bosnia, East Timor, and Kosovo, donors funded projects to renovate shattered buildings that housed newspapers or radio stations, repair existing radio and television transmitters, and install new transmitters. They also distributed transistor radios in Afghanistan to give people access to news and information. Moreover, donors provided funding to governments to pay salaries of staff and experts engaged in regulating the media industry.

Promoting Transformation of State Media

International donor agencies also support initiatives to transform state-owned media, either through privatization or through reforming the institutions into genuine public service organizations. Under the first option, the enterprise is sold to a private sector firm; the second option involves bringing it under the control of an autonomous body and reforming its practices. Under the second option, although the enterprise may continue to receive funds from the state, the newly established body lays down policy guidelines and is supposed to manage it without governmental interference. In either case, the purpose of these initiatives is to liberate the media outlet from direct or indirect government control.

USAID and its partners have assisted with the privatization of state-owned media enterprises. In the aftermath of the collapse of communist rule, most of the state-owned media enterprises in countries such as the Czech Republic, Poland, Romania, Russia, and Slovakia were privatized. Consequently, many of these enterprises have emerged as viable, profit-making firms. However, the privatization process has not been free of problems. Government officials and ruling parties often passed on these enterprises to their cronies. Although the media outlets became nominally independent, they remained subservient to the ruling parties and governments. In other cases, shrewd business and political operators managed to acquire the outlets at nominal cost to pursue their political and economic objectives. They sought the ownership not to run them as business enterprises but to exercise power. This was the case in Russia, where a few oligarchs succeeded in building large media empires, often through dubious means. President Putin has more or less succeeded in crushing these oligarchs and has gained indirect control over national television stations. Neither the rule of the oligarchs nor the Russian president's heavy grip on the major broadcasters bodes well for the cause of media freedom. In Serbia, there is genuine fear that many of the privatized municipal television stations might be taken over by criminal elements.

The ownership of state enterprises has in some cases been transferred in shares to employees in the hope that they would manage it effectively and freely. Such an approach was consistent with socialist practices familiar in those societies. When Radio 101 was privatized in Zagreb, Croatia, its shares were distributed among the station's ninety-six employees. Problems soon arose because these employees tended to be more interested in job security than generating profits. It took several years for the station to create a structure that could lead it to profitability.

Some privatized media firms were eventually acquired by foreign firms because local entrepreneurs lacked resources to purchase them or make the necessary capital investments. Broadcast media, which is technologically driven, has been highly susceptible to foreign acquisition. In many East European countries, such as the Czech Republic, Hungary, Poland, and Romania, foreign firms have acquired a major stake in the television industry. In Bulgaria and Hungary, foreign firms also own major newspapers. Many political leaders and commentators in these countries are concerned about the long-term political and cultural consequences of foreign ownership of a large section of the media.

The donor community now recognizes that considerable preparations are necessary before promoting the ambitious step of privatization of state-owned media enterprises. Precise rules and procedures should be established after a careful examination of both the long- and short-term consequences. The procedures for privatization should be transparent. Suitable mechanisms should be developed so that local entrepreneurs can raise capital, if necessary. Plans should be made about the placement of, or compensation for, surplus staff to ease the difficult process of transition.

Many European donors prefer the public service model for government-owned broadcasting stations and have provided technical and financial assistance accordingly. European governments, including the United Kingdom, and the European Commission have invested heavily in transforming state broadcasting into genuine, countrywide public service stations. Progress has been slow, however. US agencies and implementing partners remain doubtful about the possible transformation of state-owned media into autonomous public service entities. They believe that because these entities are likely to receive government funds, they would always remain beholden to government officials and political leaders. Their management boards would remain vulnerable to manipulation by government ministries and ruling parties. The underlying argument is that transitional and post-conflict societies conspicuously lack the kind of political institutions and culture that have safeguarded the professional integrity of public broadcasting entities in the United Kingdom, Germany, and Scandinavian countries. The blatant way in which state-owned media are still being manipulated in the developing world to serve partisan political interests provides little hope for the autonomy of public service broadcasting in developing and transitional societies. Perhaps the reform of state broadcasters can best be accomplished through legal and regulatory reform. Lobbying for media freedom can include calls for changing the rules and terms of governance for state broadcasters in order to limit opportunities for political interference, require public service content in programming, and mandate financial transparency.

General Observations About Media Development

Before concluding this chapter, a few general observations about media development can be made. First, media development requires multipronged efforts, affecting different aspects and facets of the media sector (see Box 2.1). A robust media sector requires journalists who are well trained and internalize the norms of free media; managers that run media outlets as sound business enterprises; outlets that are economically viable and are not dependent on outside economic or political interests to survive; advertising and audience firms that provide services to support a thriving media market; media laws that safeguard press freedom, access to public information, and fair licensing and competition; and industry associations that articulate the interests of journalists and media owners. These strategies tend to be complementary and mutually reinforcing. The ideal approach is to fashion various media interventions that focus on different elements of the media sector.

Second, the focus of development approaches depends largely on the nature of the political system. In relatively open societies, which in theory (if not in practice) guarantee political rights and freedom of the press, the international community can design and implement programs that suit that climate. For example, in postcommunist Eastern Europe, donors supported myriad projects focusing on various issues, ranging from journalism training to reforming legal and regulatory regimes. However, in authoritarian and closed societies, international donors have few options. They can undertake only those programs that would be permissible in the existing political order. Most Middle Eastern countries require drastic reforms in media law and regulation

Box 2.1 Media Development Programming Approaches

- Upgrading Journalistic Skills and Expertise
  Short- and long-term journalism training
  Training in media ethics and accountability
  Assistance to schools of journalism institutes and
    organizations
- Promoting Economic Viability
  Training in management and marketing
  Training in financial management
  In-house consultancies
- Financial Support to Selected Media Outlets
  Grants and loans
  Provision of equipment (e.g., computers, transmitters,
    software, cameras, printing presses)
  Subsidies for the sale of newspapers and magazines
  Subscriptions for news wire and photo services
- Promoting Legal and Regulatory Reforms
  Legal assistance for the drafting of media laws
  Technical and financial assistance for establishing
    regulatory bodies
  Assistance to organizations engaged in legal training to
    journalists
  Training in media laws
- Strengthening Media Organizations
  Support to journalists' associations
  Financial and technical assistance to trade associations
  Assistance for establishing audience research agencies
    and organizations
  Technical and financial assistance to journalism
    institutions
- Transformation of State-Owned Media
  Legal assistance for privatization
  Financial support for privatization
  Technical assistance to transform state media into public
    service outlets

for the emergence of a free media. Yet these countries would be reluctant to allow programs that promote such reforms because it would undermine the authority of the existing regimes. As a result, international media NGOs have to focus on journalism training and institution building. Authoritarian conditions sometimes require development strategies involving the gradual planting of seeds instead of more ambitious, confrontational approaches.

Third, as access to and control over the media is intricately related to existing power relations in a country, media assistance often can be threatening to ruling political parties, governmental bureaucracies, and even media owners who have privileged relationships with the regime. Such groups are usually concerned that international programs (particularly pertaining to legal and regulatory reforms, access to information, and privatization) could undermine their direct and indirect control over the media. Although vested interests might not oppose media assistance publicly, they remain hostile to the concept.

Fourth, like other democracy promotion efforts, media development efforts often require outside political support. Diplomatic pressure by major powers on reluctant governments is often needed to initiate legal and regulatory reforms, create a leveling field for state-owned and commercial media outlets, and protect journalists from intimidation. The problem is that such diplomatic support is generally not forthcoming except in the case of postconflict societies. Donor governments often are reluctant to spend their political capital on lobbying for media reforms because they have other urgent economic and political priorities to protect.

Finally, many transitional and postconflict countries lack political and economic institutions that foster independent media. Civil and political rights, even when guaranteed by constitutions, are often ignored and violated by those in power. The judiciary often does not enjoy genuine autonomy and therefore is not able to enforce the rule of law or the liberties granted in a constitution. Law enforcement agencies can be corrupt and under state control. Political parties' commitment to democracy is often superficial. Civil society and human rights groups sometimes lack both leadership and resources and can be ineffective as a result. Literacy rates are lagging in many such societies, with many citizens unable to read newspapers or magazines. Such countries often lack a vibrant private sector that can generate sufficient advertisement revenues for independent media outlets. The absence of a supporting political and economic environment tends to constrain media-building efforts.

However, despite the absence of functioning political and economic institutions, most developing countries tend to have civic and political organizations, opposition leaders, educators, journalists, media owners, and dissidents who cherish an independent and responsible media. Often these organizations and individuals are willing to take risks and forge partnerships with international media NGOs. International media projects have benefited by working closely with such dynamic individuals and organizations in the Balkans, Eastern Europe, and Russia. Future media projects in other parts of the world can also profit from close partnerships with indigenous prodemocracy organizations and individuals.

Notes

1. These estimates were provided by the Internal Institute of Education.
2. This finding is highlighted by an assessment of USAID's media assistance to the Russian Federation. See Kumar and Cooper 2003.
3. A six-country assessment of USAID's media assessment noted this phenomenon. See Kumar 2004, 4.
4. It should be noted that the necessary legal and regulatory reforms were more or less imposed by the Office of High Representative in Bosnia. Ruling parties had very little say in this matter and generally resisted reforms.
5. The international community made a valiant effort to bring together three journalist associations in Bosnia, which have now created a single national body called the Coordination of Journalists Association. See IREX 2003, 21.
6. For example, in Bulgaria, when the government tried to appoint a partisan director general of state radio, media associations and unions joined to oppose it and ultimately succeeded.
7. Media sustainability indexes published by IREX in 2001, 2002, and 2003 cite many examples that substantiate this observation.

3

Journalism Training and Institution Building in Central America

The overall goal of the project is to strengthen journalistic profes-sionalism . . . and do so in a manner which, in time, will enable the professional journalism community in the region itself to carry on these tasks.

—LAJP Project Proposal

This chapter presents a case study of a major independent media development intervention supported by an international donor agency in Central American countries. The Latin American Journalism Pro-ject (LAJP) was funded by the US Agency for International Develop-ment and designed and implemented by Florida International Univer-sity (FIU). For many reasons, this project is critical for understanding the nature and evolution of international media assistance. It was the first large-scale international attempt to improve journalism stan-dards and practices in developing and transitional countries. More-over, it was a long, sustained training and development enterprise; it started in the late 1980s and continued until the mid-1990s. During its life, LAJP has been instrumental in providing training to thou-sands of journalists and upgrading professional skills and expertise

This chapter is derived from a report published in 2003 titled *Journalism Training and Institution Building in Central American Countries* that Rick Rockwell and I wrote for the US Agency for International Development.

throughout Central America. Finally, the project helped to establish the Center for Latin American Journalism (CELAP), an independent, self-sustaining journalism institute.

After briefly describing the media scene at the time of the launching of the project, this chapter explains the nature and activities of the project. It then briefly discusses the establishment of CELAP and the challenges facing it. It ends with a discussion of the overall contribution of this innovative program to the growth of independent media and consolidation of democratization in Central America and outlines some policy lessons for the international community.

The Regional Media Scene

Few countries in Central America had much experience with a democratic system before the wave of democracy spread across Latin America in the late 1980s and early 1990s. Military dictators, juntas, or generals who wielded power from behind the facade of presidents and popularly elected representatives ruled Honduras for most of the previous century. When Violeta Chamorro turned over power to her successor in 1996, it was the first peaceful transfer of power in Nicaragua's recent history. In El Salvador through most of the past century, power alternated between presidents who were members of the country's agricultural elite, and leaders of the military. Although progressive elements of the country's business elite ascended into power in Panama, the country's short history is filled with military coups and dictators. Guatemala had its share of dictators and generals who seized power, punctuated by periods marked by attempts at democratic rule (Skidmore and Smith 2001). The only exception has been Costa Rica, which has enjoyed a long history of democratic government.

Although the media in these countries at times attempted to balance or confront authoritarian power, often they were established to amplify the voice of powerful authoritarian states. Usually, government coercion or subsidies persuaded most media owners to follow the government's lead. Unlike the Western democracies, most of these countries did not develop a tradition of independent advertising for mass appeal. Instead, commercial advertisers sought cues from the government on whether to support specific media outlets. Cancellations by private commercial advertisers followed withdrawal of state support (Waisbord 2000). Thus, subservience to the regime was essential for the economic survival of media outlets. Moreover, the media outlets perceived as hostile to the regime were often the targets of repression, if not outright closure. In El Salvador and Panama, governments often employed violent tactics to smother opposition media voices.

Such a system produced polarized media structures in a few countries. If the media could not find government funding, opposition political parties provided the only other regular means of support. In Nicaragua, for example, every major media outlet evolved as the voice of one or another of the country's political parties. Each party presented its own brand of media: the Liberal Party with La Noticia, Canal 2 (on television), and Radio Corporación; the Conservatives with La Prensa; and the Sandinistas with El Nuevo Diario, Radio Ya, and Canal 4 (also television). During the 1980s, the Sandinistas either appropriated or closed all the Liberal Party media outlets. In Honduras, although newspapers might have supported the various parties (Liberal or National), during the 1980s all major media outlets gave tacit support to the military, which was unchecked by presidential power until 2000. In Panama, media outlets were identified either as supporting the dictators or as opposition outlets. Opposition media were often censored or closed by the authoritarian government in Panama.

All over Central America, the standards of journalism were extremely poor. Many journalists were not qualified to cover economic and political issues. Poorly paid, they had little incentive to go after interesting stories. They were also concerned for their personal safety from the state security forces, guerrillas, and drug traffickers. The owners and publishers, often representing powerful economic and political interests, did not hesitate to interfere in news operations. Most either had a superficial commitment to the notion of editorial freedom or thought such freedom was a luxury they could not afford while supporting authoritarian political systems.

Central American journalists had a limited view of the world, with few looking beyond their national borders for stories or regional trends. Investigative reporting was practiced at very few outlets, partially due to the dependency established between the state and media owners (Waisbord 2000). Often, Central American journalists were not only deficient in their craft but also did not subscribe to professional ethics. Corruption was not uncommon both in print and broadcast media. Although there were honest, committed journalists, many—if not most—were not averse to accepting bribes from the government, military, or political parties in return for favorable coverage. Poor salaries, pervasive corruption in economic and political life, the system of political patronage, and, above all, the poor institutionalization of the norms of journalism contributed to this atmosphere where low standards were accepted. This further undermined the credibility of the press.

Most Central American countries did not have vibrant civil society organizations that supported independent media. Journalism associations were often weak and usually divided. It was not uncommon to have more than one association in a country. The owners and publishers often distrusted such associations. As a result, there was no common ground between them. Because authoritarian governments for the most part controlled the region, the rule of law was weak or nonexistent in many of these countries.

In short, the media landscape in Central American countries in the early 1980s was hardly encouraging. Most countries lacked the democratic institutions that are essential for the growth and survival of the free press. The standards of journalism were generally poor, and the quality of their output left much to be desired. It was at this stage that FIU proposed the Latin American Journalism Project to USAID.

The Latin American Journalism Project

USAID gave FIU a grant of $475,000 in 1994 to conduct an in-depth assessment of the state of journalism in Central America. The purpose was to come up with a comprehensive plan for improving the standards and practices for journalism (Heise and Green, 1996). FIU appointed a three-person research team that took six months to travel throughout the region, conducting in-depth interviews with 150 journalists, journalism educators, and media owners.

The assessment found that Central American countries lacked educational institutions capable of imparting sound journalism training. Most universities taught social communication and communication theory, but not modern journalism. The few journalism departments that existed were often highly politicized, with curricula that emphasized theory and did not provide practical instruction. No regional training center for journalism existed in the early 1980s. Only a few journalism textbooks in Spanish were available that used relevant, practical examples.

The findings of the assessment team were later discussed in a workshop held at the Florida International University. The three-day workshop included journalists, media owners, and experts from the United States and Central America. There was a broad consensus among the participants that only a long-term educational and training program would have any impact on the region. Such a program, they agreed, should have a professional and practical focus. It should use instructors from Latin America to conduct many of the training sessions, and it should take into consideration existing Latin American realities and not blindly impose the journalism practices of the United States. The workshop recommended that efforts focus on journalism training, professional ethics, news organization administration, and business management. It also recommended that an independent center, functioning on a decentralized basis throughout the region, be established to be the focal point for these activities (Green 2002). Based on the recommendations of the workshop, FIU submitted plans for a seven-year, $12 million multicountry training program to USAID. In turn, USAID funded the program for five years beginning in 1986 with a budget of $9.3 million, but later extended it for three years with an additional $4.5 million.

From the beginning, FIU was concerned about the integrity and independence of the project. During the pilot training session of journalists, FIU officials realized that the program could be controversial because of its ties to the US government. Some journalists questioned the motives behind the project. They expressed concern that the US government was funding the project to counter journalism programs being directed by Cuba and the Soviet Union, to disseminate anticommunist news stories to newspapers, or to channel funds for propaganda purposes. Some even suspected that the US government was using FIU to achieve its political objectives.[1]

Such criticisms were credible because the US government had funded journalism training projects to fight communism. For example, the Central Intelligence Agency (CIA) supported a program through the US Information Agency to train Afghan guerrillas as journalists at Boston University. Journalism training projects and funding for pro-US publications to counter Soviet propaganda were suggested by the Kissinger Commission's report to the Reagan administration. Following these recommendations, the CIA, with USAID support, funded the supplement *Nicaragua Hoy,* which regularly appeared in the Costa Rican newspaper *La Nación* (Shallat 1989). *Nicaragua Hoy* was a voice for the Nicaraguan Contras and the Nicaraguan exile community in Costa Rica during the Contra War.

FIU took several steps to allay these apprehensions and ensure the integrity of the project. First, it proposed and constituted an advisory board composed of journalists and journalism educators from within and outside the region. The board shaped the policies and activities of the program. Second, FIU insisted that the project operate in accordance with the professional principles of the free press in Western democracies. The project proposal stated, "it is imperative that the project be operated independently by Florida International University, free from political ideology and fully committed to professional principles of a free press" (Heise and Green 1996). To assure the integrity of the project, the university insisted that it have sole authority to close down the project if it was used "by anyone for purposes other than strengthening the professional news media in Central America" (Heise and Green 1996).

Third, FIU sought and gained two important waivers from USAID. The first concerned selection of participants. Patterning its selection criteria after the Nieman Fellows Program at Harvard University, FIU insisted that it should be the final arbiter. The second waiver concerned the "prepublication review" of all publications by USAID. Such review was unacceptable to FIU, as it violated the norms of press freedom (Heise and Green 1996). USAID provided both these waivers. In hindsight, efforts by FIU to ensure the independence of LAJP from political influence and USAID's full concurrence to the principle were critical factors in the success of the project.

LAJP undertook a wide variety of activities and projects to support the emergence of independent media in Central America. These can be grouped under the categories of training, publications, and networking.

Short- and Long-Term Training

As the main objective of LAJP was to improve the professional skills of journalists, it largely focused on both short- and long-term training, which was practical and relevant to Central American conditions. Its emphasis was not on theoretical discourse but on making journalists more professional and productive in their craft. Therefore, LAJP offered intensive courses on writing skills for print and broadcast journalists, news reporting, the production of television news, and the use of cameras and editing. It also supported courses on investigative journalism. In addition, it developed courses on election coverage and reporting so that journalists could cover elections with objectivity and balance. Finally, LAJP organized intensive training seminars on professional ethics. By all accounts, the project was the first organization to propose solutions to the climate of corruption in the journalism profession in Central America.

An overwhelming proportion of the training was short term, for two reasons. First, limiting the training time to two or three days enabled LAJP to maximize the number of trainees and thus program outreach. Long-term training programs would have been expensive and reached fewer journalists. Second, media owners were not willing to send their employees for long-term training. Early in the program, some journalists who attended longer training sessions returned to their home countries to discover their jobs had been given to others. Short training sessions allowed journalists a break from their routines, but not enough time for reluctant owners to have second thoughts about their absence. Given the deadline nature of journalism and the constant need to produce new journalistic products, shorter sessions allowed journalists a more flexible schedule of training opportunities.

Training sessions were held both at FIU in Miami and at the LAJP regional training center in San Jose, Costa Rica. In the latter years of the program, some of the sessions were held at CELAP's new independent training facility in Panama. The training sessions ranged from two to five days. At the height of the program, LAJP offered as many as sixty-five different training courses in a single year. None of the training courses had more than eighteen journalists at a time. Instructors for the training program were selected from among FIU faculty and journalists from Latin America and the United States.

To reduce the cost, LAJP also undertook short-term training in different countries. Under this arrangement, faculty would relocate to a central location in one of the countries of the region, and trainees would come to their location. Usually, these training courses attracted most of their participants from the host country, although sometimes journalists from neighboring countries would attend. Those attending the first round of courses were often chosen as trainers for future courses in their own countries. LAJP trainers also worked inside newsrooms to give intensive training. Sometimes, owners asked LAJP to provide trainers to act as editorial consultants and editors for extended periods. In that way the news operation became a daily workshop as journalists performed their regular tasks under the tutelage of LAJP advisers.

Finally, under arrangements with LAJP, FIU offered a special degree program (in Spanish) for Central American journalists. The objective was to prepare highly skilled journalists to serve as the leaders and teachers of journalism, an expectation that proved to be realistic. A few trainees taught courses in journalism in their countries after completion of their studies. Some of these FIU alumni were also instrumental in steering other journalists to the LAJP training program. The project funded 126 trainees for the FIU degree program.

Trainees were screened by representatives of the program in each country and by a committee of faculty members at FIU. Only full-time journalists who had the consent of their employers could apply for the training. Questions were raised about selection of the participants. The assessment revealed that some journalists felt the selection process—although removed from the politicized process of review by the US Embassy or USAID—could have been more transparent and open. In addition, it relied on a few advisers who were not always fair.

Altogether, LAJP provided training to more than 6,800 participants (see Figure 3.1). These figures are slightly misleading, as the project counted the number of trainees in each training course irrespective of whether participants had attended earlier courses. Since many journalists might have participated in more than one course, the actual number of the participants is likely to be less.

Publications

LAJP initiated a number of publishing projects to support its training initiatives and help other educational institutions. These publications also helped develop and strengthen networks among journalists and interested media institutions. In 1990, LAJP created *Pulso,* a journalism review for the region, to cover critical issues concerning journalism training and education. The magazine became a forum for discussions and elaborations of journalistic techniques and standards. It generated advertising revenue that was used to finance CELAP, the training institute that followed LAJP. Although the magazine stopped publishing hard copy when USAID support ended, FIU keeps an electronic version of *Pulso* alive at www.pulso.org. This version of *Pulso* is financed with support from the Robert R. McCormick Tribune Foundation.

Another popular venture of LAJP was the *Latin American Media Directory,* first published in 1993. The purpose of this directory is to provide necessary information about media institutions and journalists and to promote interactions among them. This publication was supported with advertising from publishers throughout the hemisphere.

Figure 3.1 LAJP Participation, 1988–1998

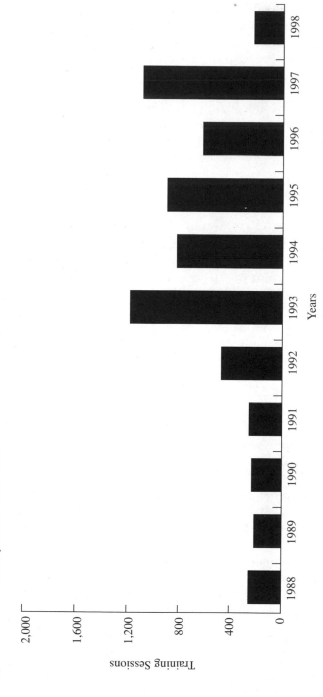

Note: Totals are the number of participant sessions, not the total numbers of participants. Totals include CELAP activities in 1997 and 1998 and registrants for CELAP's first Congress of Latin American Journalists in 1997. Total participant sessions: 6,838.

Like *Pulso,* the directory is now issued electronically; it is available at www.mediaguia.com. Some of the proceeds from directory sales were earmarked to finance CELAP.

Finally, LAJP was instrumental in creating Spanish-language textbooks for journalism education. Portions of the proceeds from the sale of textbooks were set aside to support CELAP. Altogether, the program published ten texts under the series title Journalism in Latin America. They cover a variety of topics, including ethics, writing, investigative reporting, television and radio production, interviewing, and business reporting.

Annual Awards Program

One of LAJP's most innovative initiatives was the establishment of the Premios de PROCEPER annual awards program in 1992 to honor outstanding journalists. These awards also honored journalists willing to take on controversial and important investigative projects. Many award recipients were journalists who investigated death squads and extrajudicial killings by militaries in the region. The awards ceremonies were often broadcast regionally and featured prominent speakers such as some of the presidents of Central American countries. The awards also built interest in the LAJP and FIU training programs. Journalists from every country in the region were honored during the six years the awards were presented. The awards program ended with the end of LAJP.

Conferences

The project also organized a number of conferences, covering topics such as employer/employee relations; increasing profitability of news organizations; university entrance, graduation, and media employment for journalism students; raising the stature of the profession; conflict of interest; and corruption. Such conferences helped build a regional network and enabled journalists, owners, and educators to exchange information and ideas. It also promoted regional dialogue on common problems facing the media sector.

Code of Conduct for Journalists

After extensive informal discussions, LAJP ultimately succeeded in its efforts to establish a code of conduct for journalists. In 1993 a meeting of journalists and media owners in New Orleans, Louisiana, produced the first ethics code for journalists in the region. The code was widely disseminated by LAJP. Although no empirical evidence is available, journalists have suggested that the code helped reduce journalism corruption in Honduras (Rockwell 1998b) and Panama (Rockwell 1998c).

A few limitations of the programs were highlighted by the USAID assessment (Janus and Rockwell 1998). First, LAJP focused most of its efforts on newspaper journalism in the region. LAJP's own analysis in 1993 showed that it had trained almost twice as many newspaper journalists as broadcast journalists (Heise et al. 1993). However, in most of the countries (Guatemala, Panama, Honduras, and El Salvador), newspapers remain an elite form of media, reaching less than 10 percent of the populace on a regular basis. Thus, the major focus on print media limited the impact of LAJP on the overall media system in some countries. Two factors particularly contributed to limited focus on the broadcast media. First, the media owners who supported the project mostly owned newspapers. As a result, they encouraged their journalists to avail of the training. Second, the project found it difficult to locate radio and television facilities where intensive classes could be conducted.

Second, LAJP worked mainly with mainstream urban media outlets. Journalists from small community outlets were often underrepresented. Often, they felt structural barriers. They did not learn about the program. Their newspapers were also not willing to depute them for training as it might interrupt their normal operations. Moreover, some of these outlets felt that LAJP did not address their needs or audience (Janus and Rockwell 1998). The project did not make special efforts to attract journalists from small communities and rural areas. Considering the rural nature of much of Central America, more focus on rural outreach probably would have yielded significant results.

Finally, the assessment also noted that the project did not build a strong network of alumni trainees (Lazar et al. 1991; Janus and Rockwell 1998). LAJP did not have a strong database of alumni. A stronger organization of LAJP alumni could have helped with the transition to CELAP's management of the training initiative. Further, an alumni base could have been tapped to deal with social problems facing journalists, such as the physical dangers that still threaten journalists in Guatemala, or the oppressive criminal libel laws in Panama that have resulted in heavy fines or the jailing of journalists.

The Center for Latin American Journalism

One of the objectives of LAJP was to transfer responsibility for journalist training and other activities to an independent center directed by journalists and media owners from Central America. As there was no regional journalism institution in Central America, the leaders of LAJP were confident that they would be able to raise necessary funds and build widespread support for the planned center.

LAJP established a tax-exempt, not-for-profit foundation, the Press Freedom Foundation, chartered in the state of Florida. The foundation was formed to raise resources, establish CELAP, and transfer its leadership and management to a Central American board of directors. Its bylaws stressed that the center would follow the free-press norms of Western democracies, and its activities would be conducted independent of any government. Moreover, it would focus on both the print and broadcast media. The bylaws also stipulated that the center's board of directors should include journalists, media owners, and media educators.

LAJP took several steps to raise resources for CELAP. First, it mobilized all its earnings and marked them for the endowment. For example, it transferred all the royalties and profits from the sales of the ten books it had published as well as the advertising revenues from the journal to the endowment. It also diverted profits from the Central American media guide to the fund. Second, it contacted major foundations in the United States for assistance. Its efforts did not succeed, however. Third, the leaders of LAJP personally approached every newspaper, radio station, and television station in the region to solicit funds.

After persistent efforts, LAJP obtained written pledges of $700,000 from media owners in the region (Green 2002). A large portion of funds was generated in Panama, where major newspapers and a major television and radio holding company contributed more than $258,000. Unfortunately, many media owners in other countries failed to keep their promises. In 1996, with pledges totaling more than half the necessary endowment of $1.5 million, the leaders of LAJP decided to move forward and establish CELAP in Panama City. The center emerged as an independent entity, with its board of directors mostly from Central America, and with Roberto Eisenmann Jr. as its first president. CELAP now has a permanent staff of four including the executive director, who is responsible for its operations. There is little doubt that the center is understaffed. The small staff has to coordinate the logistics of training across the hemisphere, organize the center's biennial congresses, recruit, market, and raise funds. The leaders of CELAP recognize that the staff is overworked and underpaid.

The main achievement of CELAP is carrying on the journalism training mission started by LAJP. Since 1998, the center has had 4,122 registrants for events (see Figure 3.2). CELAP still tracks the total number of those registered (including participants in its congress gatherings) in the way LAJP did, but it also keeps a separate tally for the number of individuals involved in those events. According to its records, CELAP has had 1,268 participants at its various events, including workshops, seminars, and the biennial congress for Latin American journalists. In 2001, the center counted 778 participants in seventeen seminars conducted in seven countries and at the center's congress in Panama. This was an increase in the number of activities from 2000, when the center held eleven seminars.

Although the center attempted to publicize its training programs throughout Latin America, the appeal of the center was spread thinly around the hemisphere. For example, the participation figures for 2001 reveal that CELAP's real success has been its appeal to Panamanian journalists. Although representatives of seventeen countries and territories attended its programs, 80 percent of those attending were Panamanian. Only 7 percent came from other Central American nations, and the remaining participants came from elsewhere in Latin America.

CELAP's training programs tend to be shorter than those that were offered by LAJP. Many are one-day seminars or are held over a weekend or three days. Only a few have lasted more than a week. Although CELAP has provided fewer training options, some of the topic areas have been more specialized than the menu offered by LAJP. Recent topics for training seminars have included investigating corruption, freedom of information acts, investigative reporting, medical writing, banking laws, radio news production, and environmental and economic journalism.

A persistent problem is that CELAP expects most participants to pay for training. The cost of a typical weekend seminar is about $600 (Janus and Rockwell 1998), an amount equal to two months' salary for a journalist in many Central American countries. As a result, media owners are not enthusiastic about sending their journalists to the seminars. Journalists in El Salvador, Guatemala, and Honduras have complained about the high costs of the training activities (Janus and Rockwell 1998).

Figure 3.2 CELAP Participation, 1998–2002

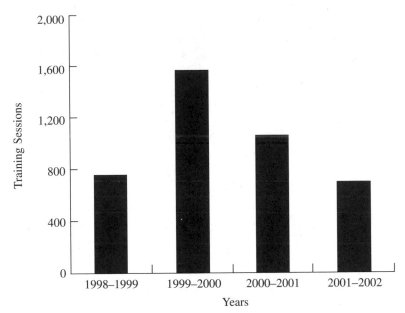

Note: Totals are the number of participant sessions, not the total numbers of participants. Totals include registrants for CELAP's hemispheric conferences in 1999 and 2001. Total participant sessions: 4,122.

CELAP has held three biennial meetings of journalists from around the hemisphere. Two of the meetings were held in Panama (1997 and 2001) and one in Puerto Rico. These meetings have been important for networking among journalists and have made CELAP quite well known in many countries. The meetings also generated $77,409 for CELAP (including a $10,000 donation from El Nuevo Día).

The major challenge before CELAP is to attain financial sustainability. Some of its board members are circulating a plan to raise an additional $1.5 million. Half of this total would be used to bring the endowment up to the level originally set by LAJP to sustain the center. The renewed fundraising plan calls for $100,000 to purchase desktop computers, video editing stations, digital cameras, and other technical equipment for the center's training room. This fundraising plan also earmarks more than $400,000 to fund the necessary cash outlays for the center's congress meetings for the next decade. The remaining funds would be used for training scholarships and to support travel for trainers.

CELAP remains a struggling organization with an uncertain future. It has the potential to become a sustainable organization that contributes to the growth of a free press in a volatile region. However, if it is unable to raise resources, it may have to close its operations.

Contributions of the Project

The overall contribution of LAJP can be examined with reference to its impacts on professional competence and skills, journalistic ethics, and the democratization process.

Professional Competence and Skills

Surveys conducted by the USAID evaluation team (Janus and Rockwell 1998) and interviews with observers of the Central American media scene indicate that LAJP made a major contribution toward improving the technical and professional skills of journalists. There has been an improvement in the quality of news reporting and editing, which should be at least partly attributed to the activities of LAJP and CELAP.

LAJP contributed to improvements in the design, layout, and coverage of many prominent newspapers in the region. The influence of LAJP can be seen in the reengineering of *El Diario de Hoy* in El Salvador (Janus 1998a), and *La Prensa*'s modern design in post-Noriega Panama (Rockwell 1998c). *Siglo Veintiuno* in Guatemala credited LAJP with improving its design (Rockwell 1998a). As a result of their new layout and better news coverage, all these newspapers increased their market share (Rockwell and Janus 2004). In Nicaragua, the project was responsible for improving the quality of news broadcasts by some independent radio stations (Janus 1998b). Radio reporters and producers in both Guatemala and Panama also credit LAJP for some of the content improvements of their news programs (Rockwell 1998a, 1998c).

Both LAJP and CELAP have directly and indirectly contributed to upgrading journalists. They trained thousands of journalists in editing, reporting, investigative journalism, news management, and camera operation. LAJP alone held training sessions for 6,800 journalists. Since 1999, CELAP has had 1,268 participants in a variety of events (workshops, seminars, and conferences). The sheer number of participants is a reasonable indicator of the impact the two organizations have made on the media sector. It should be recognized, however, that since 2002, CELAP has not been able to undertake significant training programs.

LAJP and to a limited extent CELAP have also made journalists and media owners aware of the need for training and its benefits. Trainers and alumni from LAJP and CELAP programs have spread their philosophies about journalistic ethics, investigative journalism, and journalistic balance throughout Central America and beyond during the past fifteen years. Their personal examples are cited in many of the positive anecdotes about the programs. The LAJP awards program was often referred to as the Central American Pulitzers, and winners of these awards were often regarded as leaders and trendsetters for journalists.

Awareness of the benefits has created a second wave of training programs in some parts of the region. In Guatemala, various alumni of LAJP created new training initiatives attached to local universities, journalism organizations, or NGOs (Rockwell 1998a). The positive results of LAJP and CELAP have encouraged other institutions to initiate or expand training programs in Central America or to support training programs in other countries aimed at Central American journalists. Among these organizations are the Poynter Institute (based in St. Petersburg, Florida); the Freedom Forum; the Inter-American Press Association; International Center for Advanced Studies in Journalism for Latin America (CIESPAL); the National Association of Hispanic Journalists (NAHJ), a US-based organization for Latino journalists; the International Federation of Journalists; and Northwestern University (Rockwell 1998a, 1998c). Thus the work of LAJP and CELAP has helped institutionalize training within the region and created an environment where other groups will find fertile ground for training initiatives.

Both trainees and trainers have benefited from these programs. LAJP was regarded in Central America as a prestigious training program that could make the difference in getting a job. Media outlets sought program participants for open positions. Often, listing participation in an LAJP training course on a résumé could help an alumnus land a job. Many LAJP alumni have acquired leadership positions in the region's media. Like trainees, trainers also profited from their association with LAJP. Prominent media outlets often invited them to consult. For instance, the Salvadoran newspaper *El Diario de Hoy* employed Lafitte Fernandez, an LAJP trainer, to revamp it. In Panama, Gustavo Gorriti, another former LAJP trainer, reinforced an already vigorous investigative reporting team at *La Prensa*. Gorriti's investigative reporting team was responsible for *La Prensa*'s reputation as one of the best newspapers in Latin America (Alves 1997).

Professional Ethics

A major focus of LAJP's activities was improving the lax ethical standards of the profession in the region. The leaders of the project raised the issue of professional ethics in their formal and informal meetings with journalists, media educators, and media owners. Every year, the project conducted several training courses on this sensitive issue. One of the major contributions of LAJP was bringing media owners and journalists together in New Orleans in 1993 to produce the first regional ethics code for Central America. CELAP continues to organize training activities on corruption and professional standards for journalists.

Their efforts had some positive effects on the problem of corruption in the journalism profession. LAJP highlighted the problem, made journalists discuss it, and encouraged them to rise to higher standards. The ethics code promoted by LAJP was instrumental in bolstering anticorruption programs to eliminate journalistic graft in Honduras in 1993 (Rockwell 1998b) and in Panama in 1995 (Rockwell 1998c). During the mid-1990s the new code was an inspiration for journalists fighting to clean up the profession.

Many factors and conditions have tempered the initial impact of LAJP and CELAP on corruption in the journalistic profession. First, there is an all-pervasive culture of corruption that is deeply embedded in the social and economic institutions of Central American countries (Transparency International, 2001). Unless major changes are made in the institutional environment of these countries, it is difficult to change the normative structure in the journalism profession. Second, pay scales of working journalists are relatively low. Journalists often have to struggle to earn a reasonable standard of living. As a result, quite a few succumb to the temptation to accept monetary rewards in exchange for favorable reporting. Living and working conditions of the journalists have to be improved to have a significant effect on corrupt practices. Third, media owners and managers are generally indifferent to the problem. Often tied to special economic and political interests, they do not give the problem the priority it needs.

Effects on the Democratization Process

As mentioned above, LAJP was launched in Central America as a wave of democracy was sweeping the region. Many prolonged civil wars had come to a resolution. Ballots, not bullets, had become instruments for changing governments. These changes created a new era for the media. Governments were forced to abolish censorship and their control over the media. The emergence of democracy required public access to information. There was a widespread awareness of the need for free and responsible print and broadcast media. Under these conditions the training provided by LAJP became both timely and relevant.

LAJP contributed to the democratization process directly and indirectly. By helping journalists and media outlets improve their technical and professional standards, it prepared them for their role in a democratic society. Prior to taking LAJP's training programs, the majority of Central American journalists were poorly trained and lacked an understanding of the role of the press and the professional obligations of journalists within a free society.

In El Salvador, Guatemala, Nicaragua, and Panama, where post-conflict elections were held to pave the way for peace and democracy, LAJP provided intensive training to journalists for covering elections. It ran country-specific courses, teaching journalists the norms of free and fair elections, the need for balanced coverage, and their role in monitoring electoral events. In all these countries, media training helped improve not only the conduct of the elections but also the political dialogue among competing political parties. Compared to the 1970s and 1980s, before LAJP and the wave of democratization, political discourse and elections showed marked improvements. CELAP has continued training in this area. It has encouraged in-depth coverage of one Panamanian presidential election and a national plebiscite on constitutional changes for elections.

LAJP helped newspapers that had been closed down by authoritarian regimes. For example, Panama's national guard had closed *La Prensa* and ransacked its offices and publishing plant. After the US invasion of Panama, the program helped with the recreation of *La Prensa*. The paper served as an important voice in the reconstruction of Panamanian democracy.

In addition, the investigative training and ethics codes of LAJP spawned investigative reporting teams at *La Prensa* and other publications. LAJP was cited as a reason the teams came together. Those investigative teams exposed the connections of candidates to drug cartels, bringing greater transparency to the election process in the 1990s. In Honduras, one of the program's alumni, a Premios de PRO-CEPER winner, used a series of investigative reports to expose some of the ties between the military and the death squads that had terrorized the country in the 1980s. Journalists trained by LAJP worked to explain the historic changes and shifts in the governments of the region in the 1980s and 1990s. Their reports were instrumental in letting people know about the covert activities of governments during the authoritarian past. In Guatemala, journalists helped galvanize a public response to oppose attempts to return to that authoritarian past.

Although LAJP and CELAP have made contributions to the region's march toward democracy, their limitations in shaping the democratization process should not be ignored. Training programs alone cannot transform the media into an instrument of democratic transition and consolidation. In Central America—as in many other parts of the world—the media face many structural barriers and problems that prevent them from playing a more effective role in promoting democracy and individual freedom. These include limited advertising revenues, deficient media laws and regulations, weak judiciaries, state control of the electronic media, oligarchic ownership structures, a subculture of self-censorship created by authoritarian rule, and sensationalism brought on by overcompetition in small media markets (Rockwell and Janus 2004). Because LAJP and CELAP are unable to remove these barriers, their impact on the growth of independent media and the democratization process is bound to remain limited.

Factors Affecting the Performance and Impacts of LAJP and CELAP

Several factors contributed to the success of LAJP and, to a lesser extent, of its successor, CELAP. Perhaps, the most important has been leadership. The leaders of the program were visionary, innovative, deeply committed, and, above all, outstanding managers. They were extremely well informed about the conditions in the region, and they established a remarkable rapport with the journalists, media owners, and educators. They made bold decisions and were not afraid of taking risks. Another factor was LAJP's attempt to involve Central American stakeholders. FIU constituted an advisory board consisting of media owners, journalists, and educators to guide the project. It selected members who were both committed to the program and willing to give their time to its activities. By reaching out to leaders of the Central American journalism and media community, LAJP established credibility in the region, guaranteed the participation of journalists in training programs, and attracted journalists to its training courses. CELAP has also succeeded in involving different stakeholders in its programs.

Still another factor was LAJP's professional integrity and independence. As mentioned earlier, many educators and journalists in the United States and Central America were concerned that the project was a subtle attempt by the US government to infiltrate the media and engage in anticommunist propaganda. By seeking written guarantees from USAID and assuring the public that FIU would close the project in case of interference by the government, LAJP established its credentials. The openness and transparency of LAJP convinced journalists that the program was not tied to a propaganda effort but rather represented a genuine effort to improve journalistic standards in the region. LAJP could involve the Central American stakeholders because it did not compromise its integrity and independence.

Another important contributing factor was the relevance of LAJP training to the needs of journalists and media owners. LAJP fashioned a training program that focused on practical skills relevant to print and broadcast media. It offered courses that taught elementary skills as well as advanced topics such as investigative journalism and electoral coverage. It offered both short- and long-term training programs to suit the needs of different journalists. To make training more accessible, it conducted programs in various countries. LAJP supported the journal *Pulso,* which became a significant journalism review for Central and Latin America. *Pulso* allowed communication with a wide journalistic community and amplified the LAJP's support of professional standards and ethics codes. *Pulso*'s role as a journalism review also kept LAJP abreast of issues and needs in the journalism community. CELAP has been following the example of LAJP in developing courses that impart practical skills to journalists. Because of LAJP's large and assured funding, it not only organized a range of training courses but also funded a relatively large number of journalists. It did not have to charge for its courses, a luxury CELAP could not afford. In retrospect, because it did not ask beneficiaries to share training costs and could cast a wide net for recruitment, it established a tradition that has been difficult to match.

The long-term stability of the project also contributed to its success. LAJP originally was planned as a seven-year training initiative, but it was first funded for five years and then extended for three more. As a result, it functioned as a stable organization for nearly a decade, enabling it to take a long-term view of its activities. It could recruit more qualified staff, as they were assured of long-term employment. This also enabled the project to experiment with new ideas and approaches and learn from experience. Because of its long-term stability, LAJP could develop and implement plans for the establishment of CELAP.

Above all, the timing of LAJP was critical to its success. The project went into operation when the democratization process created unprecedented opportunities for the growth of independent media in Central America. The project contributed to and benefited from the march of democracy.

To sum: Although LAJP and CELAP have made significant contributions to upgrading professional skills of journalists, its limitations in shaping the growth of independent media should not be ignored. Training programs alone cannot transform the media into an instrument of democratic transition and consolidation. In Central America—as in many other parts of the world—the media face many structural barriers and problems that prevent them from playing a more effective role in promoting democracy and individual freedom. These include limited advertising revenues, deficient media laws and regulations, weak judiciaries, state control of the electronic media, oligarchic ownership structures, a subculture of self-censorship created by authoritarian rule, and sensationalism brought on by overcompetition in small media markets. These constraints have limited LAJP's and CELAP's contributions to the growth of independent media and the democratization process.

Note

1. Guillermo Martinez of the *Miami Herald* removed himself from the informal advisory panel of the FIU project because he feared the program might have ties to the CIA. An article in the now-defunct *Miami News* quoted USAID sources as saying the program was meant as a direct counter to Soviet propaganda and policies in Central America.

4

Promoting Independent Regional Television Stations in Russia

The most important lesson from these [regional television] stations is that enterprising young Russians respond to new economic opportunities. Believe me, most owners started them not to promote democracy but to make money . . . [but] this does not mean that these stations are not contributing to press freedom in Russia.
—a Russian journalist[1]

The previous chapter presented a case study of an international project that largely focused on print media and targeted journalists for short- and long-term training in Central American countries. This chapter describes a major media assistance project designed to encourage the growth of independent regional television stations in the Russian Federation. The project deserves special study for many reasons. It focused on training journalists as well as station owners and managers, promoting commercial profitability for participating stations and building media organizations to articulate broadcasters' interests. Thus it followed a comprehensive approach to media development. Moreover, the project was launched in a country undergoing

This chapter is based on an assessment conducted by Laura Randall Cooper and Krishna Kumar of the USAID media assistance program in Russia. The full report, *Promoting Independent Media in Russia,* by Kumar and Cooper, was published in 2003.

a dramatic political transition with global implications. The stake of the international community in the success of the project was greater than in programs carried out in Central American countries. The project is still operating and has served as a model for similar efforts in Eastern Europe and Eurasia.

This project, known as the Independent Television Project, was launched by the Internews Network (an international nongovernmental organization) in 1992 with financial support from the US Agency for International Development. The project has contributed to the emergence of about 1,000 regional television stations that are economically viable and generally profitable. These stations largely rely on advertising and sponsorship for their survival and growth. The profit margins for the stations in large cities have been quite encouraging. A majority of the stations produce news and have trained editorial staff (Internews Network 2002, 15). Most of the stations are related to various media groups or holding companies in much the same way that local American stations are affiliated with national networks. This chapter describes the conditions under which the project was launched, explains the different activities undertaken, and sheds light on the factors that have contributed to the project's success.

Background of the Project

Under the communist regime that held power from 1917 to 1991, the media was under absolute state control. Soviet leaders understood the role of mass media in mobilizing people for revolutionary change, legitimizing their tenuous hold over the vast and diverse country and promoting communist ideology at home and abroad. The totalitarian regime controlled the media through complete state ownership, enforcing strict censorship, and, most important, institutionalizing a system that mandated self-censorship by journalists. The regime also centralized the media; information flowed from Moscow to the union's constituent republics and states. Obsessed with the destabilizing effects of information and ideas emanating from abroad, the regime took every possible step to impose a blockade on outside influences, although not always successfully.

As communist rule unraveled, a law on media was adopted in 1990 that opened up the formerly closed system. It guaranteed freedom of press, abolished censorship, and, in tandem with other measures to encourage privatization, recognized the right to establish privately owned media. The law also provided for the independence of editorial bodies and journalism collectives, but not for enforceable rights of access to information. It was a watershed for freedom of expression after decades of repression.

The government allowed the partial privatization of Channel 1, creating a new television giant, ORT. Although the state still owned 51 percent of its shares, the rest was passed to a consortium of banks and other industrial interests. The central government in Moscow retained control of Channel 2 (RTR). Within the country, each administrative region had its own local government-run television stations. In the early 1990s, the stations were technically under the control of the Federal Ministry of Press and Information, but were practically the "arms of regional governments" (Johnson 1993, 3).

In the mid-1990s, independent local television stations sprouted up all over the country. Most of these stations, especially in small towns and villages, had their origin in cable stations that generally served housing complexes. As these complexes were wired with master antenna systems, enterprising entrepreneurs connected them to video players, establishing rudimentary cable stations. Such stations worked in dilapidated offices with one S-VHS editing suite and three to nine cameras. They were rarely close to the transmitter facilities, and carried their tapes to a VCR located at the transmission site (Johnson 1993). Most of them showed pirated Western movies that then enjoyed immense popularity. Many of these stations had some news programming but did not employ full-time journalists and relayed news gathered from local and national media. The conditions were slightly better in large cities, where stations tended to have full-time journalists on their staff.

As the country lacked a private sector, most managers of independent stations lacked business and management experience. As a result, even the large television stations lacked a coherent management structure. Managers often improvised and formulated ad-hoc personnel policies and programming schedules. Moreover, the managers had practically no experience in advertising. They had no idea how to approach potential advertisers, create suitable advertising, or place an advertisement. But what these managers and owners lacked in experience, they made up for in determination to learn and succeed.

Project Activities

It was against this backdrop of dramatic change that Internews designed and initiated the Independent Television Project in 1992. From its inception the project was supported by USAID, which provided

$18.11 million between June 1992 and September 2002. In addition, USAID sponsored specific activities. The rationale for focusing on independent regional television was abundantly clear. These stations desperately needed outside technical assistance to survive and grow. Practically all suffered from a lack of journalistic and management skills and expertise. More important, the managers and owners were young and dynamic and eager to learn from Western experience. There were political considerations as well. It was easier to focus on regional than national media, as the federal government was not so interested in exerting control over regional television stations. Indeed, the central government welcomed the growth of independent broadcast media in the regions as it presumed regional media would be more supportive of economic and political change. Russian society was in political and social ferment, and the end of totalitarian rule provided ideal conditions for media training and assistance.

Initially the project focused on the training of broadcast journalists and station operators. However, while reviewing the effectiveness of its training programs, Internews found that its trainees were not able to make use of the skills and knowledge they had acquired. They met with resistance from station managers who were skeptical of new methods and ignorant of the techniques of broadcast journalism. To them, some of the practices that their journalists wanted to introduce were almost "revolutionary" in nature. Internews decided that the best solution was to train the managers along with the journalists.

Internews also recognized that the newly established television stations could not survive—much less uphold the principles of a free press—unless they were financially viable, operating as profitable business enterprises and employing sound management practices. As a result, the project started a new series of training seminars covering station management, accounting, advertising, and sales. In addition to traditional training seminars involving several dozen participants at once, broadcasting consultants visited stations on a much more focused and intensive basis.

After a base of stations with a clear understanding of news production, programming, and advertising began to emerge, the project broadened its focus to provide other stations with shared programming. Internews assisted with the production and distribution of programs that could be used by regional television stations. From early on, Internews worked to improve the institutional environment for the growth of independent broadcast media.

Training Programs for Broadcast Journalism

Internews began by organizing five-day seminars designed to teach basic broadcasting and journalism theory, skills, and techniques. Most were held outside Moscow, in different regions. Although originally program managers depended on Western trainers, they later found experienced Russian television professionals to conduct the seminars. The use of Russian professionals cut the cost of the training, thereby enabling program managers to provide training to a larger number of journalists within the same budget.

A typical broadcast training seminar included a short course in theory, followed by the basics of television journalism—the power of pictures, writing text to pictures, interviewing techniques, camera and sound skills, and editing techniques. Classes numbered approximately twenty participants and were led by two trainers. The program and the local host station provided the equipment. Each course combined a reporter with a camera operator. Trainees participated in a real-life newsroom atmosphere, looking for local stories to cover, with trainers acting as executive producers or news managers.

In addition to such seminars, the project developed advanced training seminars on investigative journalism, television news magazine production, political reporting, election coverage, and legal issues related to news gathering. Seminars on investigative reporting taught the trainees how to cover sensitive issues in-depth, such as human trafficking, child pornography, offshore investment, and capital flight. Russian journalism organizations such as the Agency for Investigative Journalism and the Guild for Court Reporters also assisted in the training.

Due to the varied forms of political pressure in Russia and a widespread unfamiliarity with media law in the country, Internews supported legal training seminars. These seminars were largely conducted in conjunction with organizations such as the Moscow Media Law and Policy Center (MLPC) (later renamed the Institute for Information Law, IIL) and the Glasnost Defense Foundation (GDF). Internews also organized seminars to teach broadcast journalists about election coverage and reporting.

The training program has not been without problems. Some participants thought that short-term training programs were not enough to impart necessary skills. There were also questions about the qualifications of the trainees and the selection process for recruiting them. As regional television journalists had rapidly grown more sophisticated in their news production techniques, the need to continue the seminars was called into question.

Internews also operated a five-week (since 1999, four-week) journalism school. The school went beyond basic techniques, providing select groups of promising journalists with advanced instruction on broadcast journalism. It brought practicing journalists from all over Russia and abroad to teach courses in reporting, camerawork, and editing, as well as supplemental courses on journalistic ethics, legal issues, and investigative projects. Each session of the journalism school had one primary trainer and included ten to fifteen guest lecturers speaking about specialized aspects of the television industry.

There is little doubt that the school's training programs upgraded the skills and expertise of the regional stations. Moreover, the contacts established between participants proved beneficial to their professional development. These seminars also provided opportunities for host stations to highlight the work of sister stations on their newscasts on an informal basis, with students often taking copies of stories back home to air on their own stations.

Improving Management and Financial Viability

The management seminars imparted instruction on modern management techniques, newsroom management, and capital investment. These seminars were conducted in the same manner as the training seminars on broadcast journalism. Managers from Western or Russian stations of similar size and with similar development challenges spent several days or weeks recreating real-life scenarios and using case studies from the stations to explore various management and financial issues.

In addition, the project conducted training seminars on marketing and advertising. Such training proved essential because the survival of a station largely depended on its advertising revenues. These training programs proved extremely popular, attracting the largest number of trainees with the exception of broadcast journalism classes. Closely related to these were training seminars on design and promotion, as the stations needed to create an attractive television station design.

Given how rapidly technology changes in the broadcast industry, the program provided training to stations to improve skills and technology on a regular basis. When an independent station was launched, it usually began with the most inexpensive equipment it could obtain. The use of such equipment did not require much training. However, once the station became more established, it had to secure better equipment to improve quality. Therefore, professional technical training was required to help stations learn to use their new equipment as efficiently as possible. Such training included camera techniques, editing, lighting, and shooting in difficult conditions.

Management training programs were prized by struggling and well-established regional television stations. From 1992 to 2002, over 10,000 people attended these training seminars.

Programming and Dissemination

Internews launched a number of initiatives to produce and distribute television programs. *Local Time* was designed as a news exchange program with twenty participating independent stations. The participating stations were required to produce a news spot, first once a month, and then gradually progressing to once a week. A story was produced and edited at the local regional station with the proviso that it must have broader interest for other towns and cities in Russia. Often the first pieces were flawed and quite raw, lacking production quality and balance. Internews's Moscow staff used the submissions as opportunities to confer with and critique the stations on both journalistic and technical issues, creating a kind of correspondence course in journalism training. These stories were assembled in Moscow with a taped anchor segment into a thirty-minute program; the finished program was sent back by satellite to the contributing stations.

In many cases, this was the first original programming many of these stations had ever aired, and the information-starved audiences responded overwhelmingly. This response provided the base the stations needed to attract attention and sell advertising. Within months, some of the more energetic stations were building on this success to begin producing their own news and analysis programs, most of which were taped at first and aired only once a week. Eventually, production of *Local Time* ended as the regional stations learned to produce and share stories without filtering them through Internews.

Open Skies was launched as a documentary distribution project to promote the broadcast of high-quality educational programming in 1994. Under this project, stations received programs free of charge. During the first year, *Open Skies* provided seven hours per week of quality documentaries to interested independent regional television stations, but the amount of programming was reduced to three hours per week in 1996. When the program was conceived, the staff envisioned distributing more Western programming, but the focus gradually shifted to domestically produced documentaries. USAID also funded the production of local documentaries through a grant from the Media Development Program (MDP). In 1998 Internews moved *Open Skies* from REN-TV to the newly established TNT network. Since the project's launch in 2000, more than 1,000 hours of documentary educational programming were shown on national commercial networks in hundreds of cities across Russia (Internews Network 2002, 34). Internews also used the program as a vehicle to overcome what it described as "an alarming trend towards isolationism that has been emerging in Russia in recent years" (Internews Network 2002, 34). *Open Skies* was initially cofunded by the Ford Foundation, and when the foundation ceased its funds, it was closed down.

Provintsia was launched in 1999 by Internews as a new form of video exchange to provide cross-regional, human interest material for morning shows and new programs. *Provintsia* started with a "circle" of seven local stations exchanging materials. Each station sent interesting stories to Internews and received in return a cassette with all the other stations' stories and the right to use them in their own broadcasts. By 2001, the number of participating stations grew to thirty-nine; some editions of the cassettes regularly contained as many as forty news feature stories.

In 2001–2002, a second circle of participating stations was created, allowing two stations from the same city to participate in *Provintsia* without receiving the same material as a competitor. The second circle now includes twenty stations. *Provintsia* programming now reaches an estimated thirty million people (Internews Network 2002, 39). The pilot project has evolved into a model much like the commercial feature syndicates and regional network news feeds that local broadcasters in the United States use to enhance the breadth of their news and information programming.

Promoting an Enabling Environment and Other Assistance

Finally, Internews promoted an enabling environment for the regional broadcasting stations. In the aftermath of the economic crisis of 1998, it promoted computerization of regional television newsrooms, improving the production quality and content of newscasts. Under this initiative, Internews gave technical and information support to 180 regional stations through the use of newsroom production software and an Internet-based information exchange. Internews also helped the broadcasters establish the National Association of Television Broadcasters (NAT). It supported existing organizations as well as encouraged the creation of new ones representing industry interests.

Contributions of the Project

There is little doubt that the Independent Television Project has made a profound contribution to the growth and success of regional television stations. Although these stations have progressed at varying rates, depending on local markets, political circumstances, and the commitment of managers, practically all of them have benefited from the programs initiated and implemented by the project.

The sheer number of trainees that received instruction is impressive. Table 4.1 shows the number of trainees who attended the training courses offered by the project, whereas Table 4.2 shows the number of trainees by year. Both show that slightly less than 12,000 trainees participated in the project.

The project has contributed to improved management at participating stations. Owners and managers of stations had little understanding of modern management and business practices when the project began. The multiple, practical training programs, in-house technical assistance activities, and the networks established under the project have enriched the managers' understanding and knowledge. As a result, they were able to improve management practices, raise advertising revenues, and improve prospects for survival. For example, the training made managers aware of the importance of market research. Many, if not most, regional stations routinely did audience surveys and had well-trained sales staff that worked with current and potential advertisers.

The project helped improve news coverage at regional television stations. In the past, most of the stations followed the old pattern of reporting, merely regurgitating official press releases and interview footage of prominent party leaders and government officials. Most of the stations lacked trained journalists, and self-censorship was pervasive. As a result of training and technical assistance, these stations expanded their coverage of news and events. Most subscribed to news agencies and made use of the Internet. They also employed journalists

Table 4.1 Number of Internews Trainees, 1992–2002

Type of Seminar	Number of Trainees
Journalism	4,661
Marketing and advertising	3,313
Management and investment	1,546
Technical	1,040
Promotion and design	651
Legal and elections	354
Journalism school	328
Total	11,893

Note: Figures may include returning students attending multiple seminars and do not include final year totals for 2002.

Table 4.2 Trainee Attendance by Year, 1992–2002

1992	144
1993	196
1994	237
1995	445
1996	186
1997	496
1998	600
1999	2,924
2000	2,577
2001	1,778
2002	2,310
Total	11,893

Note: Figures may include returning students attending multiple seminars and do not include final year totals for 2002.

on a full-time basis. Some even did investigative reporting. Many stations also provided fair coverage of political candidates during elections, breaking new ground in the Russian political climate.

However, it should be recognized that despite impressive progress, the majority of the regional stations have a long way to go before they fully institutionalize norms of broadcast journalism. Often the journalists are not well paid and lack necessary experience or knowledge to cover stories. Some journalists knowingly or unknowingly mix facts with personal opinions and do not hesitate to provide biased or one-sided coverage when it suits them. In addition, it is common for news coverage to be tilted in favor of a major advertiser.

Several factors contributed to the success of the Internews project. One is that the project focused on the relatively small segment of the media eager to receive assistance. When it started its activities, only a few dozen privately owned regional television stations existed, though their number has gradually grown. As a result, Internews could establish close and continuous relationships with these stations. Between 20 and 30 percent of the management and journalism staff of the regional stations received some form of training from the project. Moreover, the entrepreneurs who started these stations, and the journalists who joined them, were relatively young and eager to learn and profit from any assistance program available. When the project launched training efforts, they responded with enthusiasm and initiative. The project has also succeeded because of its emphasis on practical skills. It has designed training and other assistance programs that address the day-to-day problems faced by the regional stations. Internews's understanding of the Russian media scene has helped it to fashion programs that are relevant and useful to the regional stations.

Another factor is that the project appealed to the economic self-interest of the managers and journalists, and only indirectly to the idea of a free press. There has been a distinctly apolitical undertone in Internews's strategy that has made it acceptable to a wide spectrum of recipients, despite the fact that it was largely funded by USAID. The stated objective of the project was to make the trainees more professional and the television stations more profitable. Broadcast journalists attended training not specifically to learn the principles of media freedom but because they wanted to learn how to report, operate a camera, or edit a story—in short, to become better professionals. The same was true for the managers of the television stations, who attended the training programs and sought technical advice to learn about management, accounting, advertising, and other skills to increase their income and profits.

Still another major contributing factor to Internews's success was its leadership and staff. The NGO's director was a dynamic and respected figure in the broadcast community, and her staff was well trained, committed, and willing to learn. Project managers were not afraid of changing course, even during the middle of a program. Once an activity was implemented, they sought a full range of comments to assess what was working and what was failing. Internews operated less as a bureaucratic entity than as a committed educator nurturing a growing movement of independent-minded broadcasters. Its Moscow office was a way station for weary media travelers who, passing through the city for meetings or seminars, needed a place to eat or relax among kindred spirits. This effort to fashion a journalistic community by engendering personal and professional solidarity was cited by many trainees as a key component of the project's success.

It is also important to note that USAID adopted a flexible approach to funding and allowed Internews a maximum degree of operational freedom. When Internews demonstrated positive results early in its existence, USAID developed a relatively hands-off approach that gave Internews the freedom to carry out Russian solutions where an otherwise traditional US model might have failed. This policy continues.

Finally, the rapid growth of the country's private sector has contributed to the project's success. Since 1998 the Russian Federation has witnessed remarkable economic growth and entrepreneurship. Small- and medium-scale firms have appeared across the country. Many of them have started advertising, though on a small scale, to sell products and services. Moreover, national and international firms are trying to reach consumers in the countryside. The regional television stations have benefited from this economic progress. Without such growth, comprehensive training and technical assistance would not have produced such spectacular results.

Lessons

Before concluding this chapter it is important to mention a few lessons that can be learned from this successful media intervention.

First, the international donor community should place a priority on the business side of media operations. Prior to its engagement in Russia, the donor community had largely, though not exclusively, focused on journalism training and interchange. Little attention was devoted to improving the management and profitability of media enterprises. The Russian experience made donor governments and organizations aware that sound management, business practices, and sales were equally important for laying the foundation of an independent media sector. As mentioned earlier, Internews spent considerable resources to improve management and increase sales at the regional stations. It appealed more to the economic self-interest of owners and managers than to their commitment to democracy and press freedom. However, by helping the stations become profitable, Internews contributed to the growth of editorial independence. The resulting economic independence makes it more likely—but does not guarantee—that many of these stations would be able to resist political pressure and interference. The station managers and journalists indirectly came to understand how the operation of a free press becomes a cornerstone of a functioning democracy. Once the stations equated quality programming with rising viewership and increased advertising rates, they better understood the connection between an independent and professional media and a successful television enterprise.

Second, the Russian experience has highlighted a serious limitation of commercial broadcasting. The regional stations mostly concentrate on light entertainment because it attracts an audience and generates revenues. They devote little or no time to current affairs or documentary programming focusing on children, women, the disabled, the environment, or social problems. Commercialization has led to the virtual abandonment of educational programming that had characterized Russian television during the Soviet era. Thus there is a need to create incentives, through regulation or donor projects, that would induce the commercial stations to produce and broadcast educational programming. In Russia, the Soros Foundation is looking for ways to support content development on a local level to support more cultural and social programs.

Finally, recent developments in Russia indicate the paramount— and even decisive—importance of the political environment. Since 1992, there has been a serious erosion of media freedom. Citing terrorist attacks related to the Chechen conflict, political leaders have imposed restrictions on news coverage of sensitive events and sought to assert control over independent-minded media outlets. Practically all the major national broadcasting companies have come under the direct or indirect influence, if not control, of the government. Political leaders and commentators have begun questioning the role of a free media. So far, regional television stations have not been unduly affected by these developments. However, the outlook for these stations remains uncertain. Faced with political pressure, it is realistic to assume that many might practice self-censorship and seek accommodation with the authorities.

Note

1. Personal interview by the author with a prominent Russian journalist.

5

Media Assistance and Regime Change in Serbia

[Serbian president Slobodan] Milosevic was ousted by the media and not opposition parties. . . . Opposition parties could not reach consensus. They spent as much energy on internal feuds as fighting Milosevic. . . . In the final struggle the parties were bypassed. The main frontlines were the people and independent media.
—Aleksandar Tijanic,
adviser to President Vojislav Kostunica[1]

There is little disagreement that independent media played an instrumental role in defeating the Milosevic regime in the 2000 elections.[2] Alternative radio and newspapers, assisted by US and European donors, helped expose the regime's blatant abuse of power and the distortions presented by state television. Media operating outside state control enabled civil society organizations to educate voters, spread word of the opposition presidential candidate beyond the capital, Belgrade, and relay opinion polls that punctured the regime's façade of invincibility. Independent media created much of the political space in which the opposition could operate.

The United States and European governments had been providing assistance to independent-minded media in Serbia since the early 1990s. Donors provided substantial aid to many media outlets, nursed nascent media organizations, and gave material and logistical support for the production and dissemination of news. More important, when Milosevic announced presidential elections for May 2000, the donor community supported additional media programs for promoting free and fair elections. This chapter explores how international assistance helped build an independent media that played a leading role in Serbia's democratic transition. It offers a general background, an overview of the media assistance delivered, including programs for elections, and briefly explains the way in which media contributed to the overthrow of Milosevic's authoritarian rule. Challenges facing the media sector in the post-Milosevic era are also discussed.

The Milosevic Regime

By 1990, Yugoslavia was what a retired US diplomat called "a troubled but functioning multiethnic society."[3] The country had become a loose federation of six republics and two autonomous entities, which were often moving in different directions. The League of Communists of Yugoslavia, which had enjoyed a political monopoly since the founding of the country, had lost its legitimacy and following. It had practically disintegrated into eight regional parties, one each in every republic or autonomous region. With the collapse of the Soviet Union, the winds of political reform were undermining its communist legacy. And yet, there was no imminent threat to its survival. Despite simmering ethnic tensions, no popular sentiment existed for the disintegration of the country.

The country's economic health was in serious trouble. A system of participatory management, which was once hailed as a major innovation in the communist world, had failed to generate economic growth. As the Cold War receded and Yugoslavia's strategic importance faded, the flow of international assistance from East and West declined. Productivity gains in the country's traditional industries were almost nil, and fresh investment was not forthcoming. The standard of living was falling, and economic disparities between different regions were growing. The three least-developed parts of the country—Kosovo, Bosnia, and Macedonia—continued to lag behind other regions (Sell 1982, 22). Prosperous republics resented subsidizing the poor ones.

Unlike the rest of the Warsaw Pact states, Yugoslavia had acquired many attributes of a relatively open society. It had an emerging civil society and could boast of associations and organizations of intellectuals, artists, students, and social and cultural activities that were free of political control. The country also saw the growth of new political parties. People enjoyed many civil and political rights and traveled abroad. The media enjoyed a degree of freedom that was uncommon in other communist countries. The government and the communist party did not own or control most of the media outlets. In fact, the ownership was dispersed, as the media was considered a "social property." Newspapers, magazines, radio stations, and even television stations reported on local and national events within the broad ideological framework of the state. As long as they did not question the major national and international policies of the government, journalists were free to write and express their views. The one real taboo was to question the delicate ethnic and religious balance in the country.

Convulsions in the political climate accompanied the rise to power of a communist party official, Slobodan Milosevic, in 1986. Milosevic sought to exploit nationalist sentiment and fears that had been building under the surface. Serbs were the largest ethnic group in the country and lived in every republic except Slovenia. Milosevic tapped into a feeling among some in the Serb community that the republic's boundaries did not adequately reflect its true demographic composition, as many Serb-populated areas were included in other republics. Milosevic spoke of the Serbs' historical grievances, and his chauvinistic, bullying tone created genuine fear among the other, smaller ethnic groups, who feared Serb domination. Milosevic's rhetoric and actions thus strengthened the hands of more militant voices in other ethnic communities who wanted to secede from Yugoslavia.

After capturing political power in Serbia, Milosevic sought to acquire direct and indirect control of the key media outlets through legal and political manipulation. In 1987 the government acquired the Politika publishing house, which produced the daily tabloid *Politika Ekspres* and many weeklies. These publications, along with the republic's television and radio stations, became the mouthpieces of the Milosevic regime. In 1991 the government also acquired control over the Yugoslav news agency Tanjug, ending its independent news coverage and reporting. The government successfully pushed through legislation giving it authority to appoint the director-general and members of the governing board of Radio Television Serbia (RTS), depriving it of its independent status. Milosevic quickly grasped the importance of broadcasting his nationalist message over the airwaves and in newspapers. He also understood the power of the media, and prominent media outlets were gradually brought under his control by placing his friends and allies in all the top editorial jobs. They were skilled propaganda experts and were able to turn all sorts of events and even tragedy to their advantage.

The Serbian law on radio and television handed over authority to the republic to issue licenses for television and radio stations, a power formerly exercised exclusively by the federal government. Despite the dubious validity of the legislation, the Serbian government started issuing radio and television licenses to its supporters and cronies. Consequently, new radio and television stations emerged as servants of Milosevic's regime, including BK TV and TV Pink, which attracted a large audience.

Milosevic skillfully employed regime media to garner support for his ethno-nationalist policies. Radio Television Serbia became an instrument for inciting hatred and hostility toward other ethnic groups. Its distorted news coverage and biased commentaries presented a misleading picture of the wars in Croatia, Bosnia, and Kosovo. Ignoring atrocities committed by Serb militia and armies, the station played up acts of violence against Serb minorities. Little or no mention was made of the systematic ethnic cleansing conducted by Serbian militia in Bosnia or elsewhere. Serbs were portrayed as victims of a sordid conspiracy hatched by other ethnic groups with the tacit cooperation of outside powers. Most of the newspapers and magazines owned by the state or allies of the regime followed RTS's lead. Milosevic initially ignored radio but later tried to manipulate it for his political gains.

By 1995 Milosevic's campaign of intimidation and threats led to war and the secession of Slovenia, Croatia, and then Bosnia. Serbia became an international pariah as Milosevic consistently alienated the United States and European governments. International economic sanctions, political isolation, and the cost of a drawn-out war decimated the economy. Hyperinflation spun out of control. Milosevic had once attracted large crowds in the late 1980s, but as the conflict dragged on and economic misery spread, many sections of society became disenchanted with the former communist apparatchik. But he continued to cling to power.

Municipal elections in 1996, in which Zajedno, a loose coalition of opposition parties, won in nineteen constituencies, proved a watershed. The defeat dealt a major blow to the regime and undermined the credibility of state-controlled media. Despite a clear verdict, the government refused to recognize the results, which caused widespread public resentment and street protests. Popular anger was directed not only against the government but also against the media controlled by it. During ensuing demonstrations, which lasted eighty days through freezing temperatures, demonstrators ridiculed RTS and battered the headquarters in downtown Belgrade with eggs and red paint as they marched by. Ultimately, the government bowed to public pressure and recognized the election verdict. One immediate consequence of this belated victory was that the ownership of nineteen municipal television and radio stations passed to the hands of the victorious opposition.

However, Milosevic continued his policy of suppressing the Albanian majority in the province of Kosovo. Political repression led to terrorist acts by armed Albanians, who attacked Serbian officials and police. A younger generation of Albanian leaders had lost patience with peaceful methods. The Albanian-orchestrated shootings provoked more brutal measures by the Belgrade government, and a spiraling cycle of violence ensued. US and European envoys, determined not to allow a repeat of events in Croatia and Bosnia, made clear to Milosevic that the North Atlantic Treaty Organization (NATO) was ready to launch air strikes if he refused to negotiate a peace settlement in good faith. When Milosevic's representatives refused a political compromise brokered by US and European diplomats, the NATO alliance bombed Serb military bases in Kosovo. The bombing, which began in March 1999, ended in June when Milosevic accepted the alliance's terms and withdrew military forces from Kosovo. By refusing the original peace deal, Milosevic ended up acquiescing to a much more sweeping arrangement that eliminated Belgrade's authority in Kosovo.

Despite policies that led to political and economic disaster, Milosevic remained confident of his strong political base. He sought to demonstrate his legitimacy by holding early elections, requiring a dubious amendment to the constitution. The elections ended in his defeat, despite his initial attempts to suppress or alter the results of the vote. Instead of gaining legitimacy, Milosevic became an indicted war criminal displaced to the Netherlands.

International Media Assistance During the 1990s

Before discussing the nature and focus of international media assistance, two general observations may be helpful.[4] First, although their long-term goal was to promote an independent media sector, the donors clearly sought to achieve a distinct political objective. This was particularly true after 1996, when US and European governments had given up on the possibility that Milosevic might serve as a factor of "stability" after he signed the Dayton peace agreement (which ended the wars in Bosnia and Croatia). Because most donors and media NGOs saw his regime as a major impediment to the growth of independent media, they did not regard the two goals as necessarily incompatible. Nonetheless, there was a tension between these two objectives of independent media development and weakening Milosevic's hold on power. For example, often the assistance was based on political rather than economic considerations. The international community did not take into consideration the commercial viability of a media outlet in providing technical or financial aid. Moreover, the distinction between independent and opposition outlets was blurred, and editorial excellence was not always treated as the highest priority.

Second, because of the authoritarian nature of the regime and shifting international priorities, donors were unable to pursue a coherent long-term strategy for strengthening the media sector until the fall of Milosevic. The primary focus of assistance during the 1990s had been to support any independent print and broadcasting media outlets that seemed committed to notions of free press and open society. The assistance was provided in the form of financial aid, grants of equipment, training, and technical assistance. The international community also tried to help bolster some fledgling media organizations seeking to lobby for press freedom and promote professional solidarity.

Donor governments started providing media assistance in 1990, directing the aid to stations, news agencies, or publications that were already established. Between 1990 and 1995, the International Media Fund, a US-funded entity, provided equipment to the television station Studio B, the weekly magazine *Vreme,* the production company Vin, the newspaper *Nasa Borba,* and several regional media outlets. It also gave financial assistance to the radio station B92 and other projects. Simultaneously, the Open Society Foundation (OSF) also launched elaborate media assistance programs. It supported local journalists in establishing two media organizations—the Independent Journalists Association of Serbia and the Belgrade Media Center (which sought to strengthen ties between journalists and civil society). The European Union invested about €1.7 million in independent media from 1993 to 1997.

Since 1991, almost every major donor has provided assistance to Radio B92, which has acquired a kind of celebrity status outside Serbia because of its refusal to bow to Milosevic's pressure and its youthful, dynamic style.[5] B92 began as a small student radio station in May 1989 with a defiant attitude, playing cutting-edge rock music interspersed with interviews and news delivered in an often sarcastic tone. In its early years, the station was a rare voice of tolerance at a time when nationalist hysteria prevailed.[6]

The station's irreverent programming caught the attention of the regime in March 1991, when tens of thousands of people demonstrated against partisan control over state television. The demonstrators referred to Radio Television Serbia as the "Bastille." Struggling to halt the protests, Milosevic ordered army tanks out on the streets, and police temporarily took B92 off the air. Irritated by the station's irreverent pranks and bold news reporting, the authorities ordered the station to cease news coverage and confine itself to music. B92 complied with the order but continued to play songs with subversive lyrics about peace, protest, and freedom. During the Croatian and Bosnian wars, the station angered the regime with its critical attitude and its sympathetic coverage of antiwar campaigns. The station satirized state propaganda and regime figures, exposing the distorted news coverage of the state media. The authorities retaliated by banning the station a number of times, including by a decree in late 1996. But the international outcry that followed forced the regime to rescind its decision.

Although the radio station opposed the NATO bombing, the authorities took advantage of the air strikes as a pretext to close the station down and acquire its studio, name, and property in 1999. The station re-emerged as B2-92, resuming broadcasting via the Internet. The regime moved again against the station in 2000. Once again the radio went underground and started broadcasting illegally. B92 and later B2-92 have never lacked resources because of the continuous and generous assistance provided by donors. Two other prominent radio stations that have received consistent international support are Radio Index and Boom 93. Like B92, Radio Index started as a rebellious student radio station and relentlessly opposed the policies of the government. Boom 93 was based in Milosevic's hometown and was therefore a major irritant to the president. After the opposition's victory in the 1996 municipal elections, many municipal radio stations received both technical and material support from international donors. For example, USAID provided grants to twenty-nine independent radio stations following the municipal election (McClear, McClear, and Graves 2002, 102–103). Although the magnitude of assistance was modest, it helped the struggling radio stations survive, if not improve their performance.

Donors also supported the Association of Independent Electronic Media (ANEM) from its inception. ANEM started with ten founding members and by 2000 had thirty-two stations exchanging programming and broadcasting news from B92. The Open Society Foundation, USAID, the European Union, and other donors helped with the network's expansion. The effect of the network was to give B92's newscast a national audience and to strengthen solidarity among alternative stations across the country.

When several municipal television stations came under the control of opposition parties in 1996, donors started supporting local television stations as well. These stations were usually overstaffed and lacked adequate equipment. The quality of their news programming was often poor. USAID initiated grants to twenty independent television stations to help improve their programming; other donors assisted as well. As with radio, donors supported the establishment of a national television network. In June 1998, the OSF called a meeting of major donors to promote the idea. The network was designed to encourage an exchange of programs among the participating stations as well as to articulate their interests. The United States, European Union, and OSF each pledged $2.5 million for the network, ANEM-TV. Work on the network was disrupted during the NATO bombing campaign and resumed later, with the network becoming operational in 2000.

The donor community also helped numerous national and local newspapers and periodicals. Donors covered the expenses of the tabloid *Blic* since its founding in 1996 and supported the Belgrade dailies *Danas, Dnevni Telegraf,* and *Demokratija* and the weekly *Vreme*. Donors also gave grants to many small newspapers and weeklies outside Belgrade.[7]

Journalism training formed another element of media assistance packages. USAID funded the International Research and Exchanges Board (IREX) to train seventy-five radio journalists, at least one from each of ANEM's radio affiliates, in the late 1990s (McClear, McClear, and Graves 2003). A cadre of trainers was formed, and a curriculum was developed. Moreover, donors helped to establish short-term training facilities at the ANEM Training Center and the NGO Invision for broadcast, and similar centers at *Vreme* and the *Ekonomist* for print media. They also supported the Novi Sad School of Journalism, which provided long-term journalism education to interested students.

Serbia's two independent news agencies—FONet and Beta—received international technical and financial assistance. Both were started by former employees of the state-owned Tanjug news agency who were frustrated by its lack of professionalism. FONet, founded in 1993, was privately owned and specialized in audio reports and journalism. Beta, which started a year later (1994), provided comprehensive news coverage. It has since emerged as a highly professional news agency known for its accuracy and reliability.

Other international donors nurtured indigenous media organizations, including the Association of Independent Electronic Media, the Association of Private Print Media, and the Independent Journalists Association, which played important roles in campaigning for media freedom and strengthening solidarity within the media industry and profession. The Belgrade Media Center owes much to donor aid for its capital and running expenses. In addition, the international community has poured resources into numerous civil society organizations that are supportive of press freedom and human rights.

At the end of the NATO air campaign, emergency assistance was delivered to help independent media quickly resume operations. Donors held a conference in Budapest, Hungary, in September 1999 to discuss immediate and urgent needs for print and broadcast media. Consequently, many donors provided survival grants to the most needy outlets. The European Union granted €1 million, and USAID gave a slightly smaller amount.[8] IREX, with USAID funding, also distributed newsprint worth $600,000 to help local newspapers and periodicals.

Independent Media in Early 2000

During the NATO campaign against Serbia, the Milosevic regime undertook sweeping repression to stifle independent media voices. According to draconian guidelines issued by the Ministry of Information, all media outlets were expected to follow the lead of state media in news coverage and reporting. All journalists were supposed to toe the official line. "Every journalist in the field or newsroom must be at the service of the state's current interests and participate in the system of reporting and information," the decree stated. Those outlets that failed to obey were heavily fined or even closed down. The most conspicuous victim was Radio B92, which was forced to cease operations in March 1999 and was acquired by the government. The regime had also targeted independent newspapers such as *Danas, Blic,* and *Glas Javnosti.* The regime liberally used the penal code and libel laws to intimidate and punish media outlets that did not bow to the official editorial line. Frequent police raids and visits by health and safety officials reinforced the climate of intimidation and censorship.

Independent media outlets also suffered because of widespread public anger and resentment against the NATO air strikes. Many citizens perceived the bombing as unfair and unjust and were generally sympathetic to the stand taken by the government. As a result, media outlets that had received international assistance were treated with suspicion and hostility. Although independent media outlets criticized the NATO action, nationalist elements tried to portray them as servants of US and European powers supposedly plotting to dismantle Serbia. Newspapers and magazines found themselves in a precarious situation amid a widespread shortage of newsprint and heavy fines imposed by the authorities. ABC Grafika, Belgrade's independent printing house, went bankrupt as a result of government fines.

Despite these difficulties, a number of independent-minded newspapers and weeklies were still operating in Serbia in early 2000. These included three newspapers—*Blic, Dnevni* and *Danas;* the newsweekly *Nin,* which was originally part of the Politika publishing house but became independent later; and *Vreme,* founded in the fall of 1990. The two independent news agencies—FONet and Beta—were also functioning. But the circulation of independent newspapers and periodicals, which largely catered to the urban elite, was limited. Inflation had rendered newspapers prohibitively expensive.

Although over a hundred independent radio stations were functioning in Serbia, most of them did not provide news and political commentary and therefore had little impact on the political landscape. Belgrade's three prominent independent radio stations—B92, Radio Index, and Studio B—were revived in one form or the other after the difficult period of the NATO air campaign. Outside Belgrade, fifteen municipal stations covered news with varying levels of journalistic independence. In addition, seven privately owned radio stations were broadcasting news outside Belgrade. The most important development in radio was the emergence of ANEM, which was broadcasting B92 news bulletins through satellite and the Internet to its affiliate stations.

About sixty independent television stations, mostly municipal and educational, were operating. Most of them had limited technical and professional capacities and reached only small populations. Belgrade Municipal Studio B TV, which covered nearly 30 percent of the Serbian population, was an exception. Municipal television stations in Pancevo and Kragujevac had maintained reasonable professional standards.

Though wounded, most of the independent media had managed to survive a repressive campaign by the Milosevic regime. The primary credit for the resilience of the independent media rests with the courageous, determined media owners and journalists and the vibrancy of the emerging civil society; however, the value of international assistance cannot be denied. Most of the independent outlets would not have survived the crackdown that accompanied the NATO bombing without financial, technical, and political support. A psychological factor was at work as well, because the editors and producers felt reassured that they had not been abandoned despite pressures from the regime. Commenting on the contribution of donor assistance, Slavoljub Javnosti, a prominent Serbian journalist has said,

> [assistance] was very, very essential, critical at the time. If aid were not forthcoming then most of the opposition media would probably have died out. This was extremely valuable not only in the physical sense that it allowed us to print but even more important was the moral support that outside this prison that Serbia was in, there were organizations that knew and could provide support. (McClear, McClear, and Graves 2002, 32)

Media Assistance for the 2000 Elections

In July 2000, when the Milosevic government scheduled an early election, international donors launched a major effort to promote a free and fair vote. They saw the elections as an opportunity to promote a democratic transition and end autocratic rule in Serbia. Led by the United States and nongovernmental organizations, the donors designed and implemented a comprehensive program involving the training of thousands of political and civil society activists, technical and financial support to opposition political parties and pro-democracy NGOs, and a massive voter education initiative. Independent media figured prominently in the overall election strategy. According to a recent USAID assessment (McClear, McClear, and Graves 2003), donor governments and organizations focused on three complementary activities.

First, the international community worked to increase the technical and logistical capabilities of media organizations to ensure that the voters received balanced coverage of election news and information. This was critical, as the ruling coalition controlled most of the media and was determined to manipulate it to its advantage. Donors provided new transmitter tubes, antennae, and transmission lines to independent broadcast media outlets. IREX and Norwegian People's Aid even funded a "pirate" television transmitter in Belgrade that could be used in case of an emergency. Every effort was made to ensure that independent broadcasters acquire equipment and expertise that was essential for election coverage. International donors also gave financial and equipment grants to a number of independent newspapers and magazines. USAID, through its partner IREX, provided Beta and FONet with backup equipment to help them transmit news to local outlets if main sites were closed by the government.

A major innovative program supported by USAID and other donors was Pebbles, Platforms for External Broadcasting. Under this project, Radio B2-92 and ANEM TV built mountaintop transmitters in Bosnia and Romania, which could rebroadcast radio and television programs back to Serbia. Both the sites became operational before the elections. Unfortunately the Bosnian site was destroyed by fire ten days prior to elections and had to be substituted by a lower-powered FM station. B2-92 and ANEM TV also built back-up radio and television studios in Bosnia. Although, strictly speaking, it was not a program of media assistance, the US-supported Ring Around Serbia—which was designed to retransmit Western broadcasts such as Radio Free Europe to Serbia—should be noted. The program focused on FM radio signals providing news and information. Program facilities were made available by USAID to the ANEM network during and after elections.

Second, international donors gave assistance to independent media outlets for the production of news programs about the elections. The Helsinki Committee for Human Rights in Serbia prepared a list of broadcast outlets that produced quality news and information programming. Using the list, various international organizations provided substantial grants to the stations to allow them to continue news operations. Special efforts were made to ensure that the results of parallel vote counting (an attempt to expose any possible electoral fraud in ballot counting) were immediately disseminated to media outlets via the Internet.

Donors also helped independent media by funding public service announcements and sponsoring special supplements on elections. USAID also supported the local NGO CeSid to place advertisements for recruiting election monitors.

The Role of the Media in Milosevic's Defeat

By carving out political space for genuinely competitive elections at a pivotal moment, independent media contributed to the fall of Milosevic's regime.

B92 and ANEM undoubtedly played a most critical role. "B92 had the most respected news in the country but the countryside was not Belgrade. The countryside distrusted Belgrade. Ultimately the rural areas were where the downfall of Milosevic would be cradled" (McClear, McClear, and Graves 2003, 11). This was accomplished by ANEM radio stations, which rebroadcast B92 news, thereby reaching nearly 70 percent of the population. B92 developed a collaborative relationship with the British Broadcasting Corporation (BBC) to relay its news bulletins to ANEM stations. It sent its audio files to the BBC through the Internet, which in turn relayed them through satellite to more than thirty-two radio stations across Serbia. Even when B92 was shut down in May 2000, it continued to provide news to radio stations all over the country via this innovative network. Later, B92 used the Internet to "feed a satellite uplink in Bosnia that was available to anyone in Serbia with a satellite dish and which provided 24 hour a day service to local stations" (McClear, McClear, and Graves 2003, 11). Moreover, all individuals and organizations that had access to the Internet could get news directly from the website.

Two weeks prior to the September elections, ANEM TV became operational, reaching fifteen television stations throughout the country. B2-92 would produce television news every afternoon in Belgrade and send it to Bosnia by car, which relayed it to independent television stations. The Serbian government spared no effort to jam its broadcasts but failed to block it entirely. Because of its late arrival on the media scene, the influence of ANEM TV on the democratic transition appears to be limited, but nonetheless significant. Independent print media outlets such as *Blic, Danas, Glas Javnosti, Nin,* and *Vreme* were also instrumental in disseminating election news and information and influencing public opinion.

The reach and credibility of independent media during the 2000 elections is demonstrated by an independent nationwide survey that USAID commissioned in September 2002. The investigators conducted interviews with 1,008 respondents, asking a set of questions about their recollections about the media during the last few months of Milosevic rule. Some relevant findings include:

- 53 percent of respondents said they watched at least one of the programs on independent media (Mreza, Vin, B92, ANEM, and Urban).
- 73 percent of respondents reported reading one or more independent newspapers (*Blic, Glas Javnosti, Danas,* and *Vijesti*).

- 41 percent of respondents thought independent broadcast media were telling the truth most of the time, whereas only 11 percent said state-owned broadcast media were telling the truth.
- 65 percent of respondents thought that state television and radio were telling lies more often than truth on political and national issues, whereas only 14 percent thought the same about independent television and radio stations.
- 57 percent stated that independent media were the most important source of information that affected voters' behavior (i.e., helped opposition win the elections).

Although the survey results have to be qualified due to their retrospective quality and the imprecise nature of polling in transitional societies, the findings nevertheless support the general perception in Serbia during the election campaign that independent media not only were reaching a significant proportion of the population but also were seen to be a more credible source of information. Moreover, people believed that the information provided by the alternative outlets affected how they voted.

Independent media provided both name recognition and legitimacy to the opposition presidential candidate Vojislav Kostunica, who was widely known in Belgrade but was not a household name in the countryside. Most people outside Belgrade came to know about him, his policies and programs, and, above all, his prospects for winning the election mainly from independent media, as the media owned by the government and its allies mostly ignored him. For example, according to a monitoring report by the Belgrade Media Center, "In the week preceding the Election Day . . . the state run broadcast media accorded over 90 percent of time slots to the regime, while the remaining 10 percent that went to the opposition was mostly used to show it in a negative light" (Belgrade Media Center 2000). The same was also true of print media. *Politika,* the regime-friendly newspaper, ran 194 stories about Milosevic but had only sixteen stories about Kostunica in the week before the vote. This was in sharp contrast to the balanced approach of *Danas,* which ran twenty-seven stories about Kostunica and twenty-three about Milosevic (McClear, McClear, and Graves 2002). Without the coverage provided by independent media, the opposition candidate might have remained an obscure political figure in many parts of the country.

Independent-minded media undermined the perception that Milosevic was invincible and that it was not prudent to oppose his rule. Instead, alternative media highlighted the vulnerabilities and hypocrisy of the regime. During the month prior to the election, polls showed Kostunica steadily gaining ground, narrowing the gap with Milosevic. Independent media played upon these results. *Blic* prominently displayed poll results on its front pages. B92 mentioned them in news bulletins. Other independent media outlets also covered these results, which were generally ignored by the state-owned media. Such news and information affected public attitudes toward the regime, which began to look increasingly frightened of its own citizens.

Independent media also strengthened NGOs engaged in promoting free and fair elections. Many prodemocracy NGOs, such as CeSid, G17, and Otpor, were instrumental in educating prospective voters about the elections, raising awareness of political rights, and mobilizing them to go to the polls. In the absence of strong political parties, these NGOs fulfilled roles that are usually undertaken by parties in democratic societies. Independent media helped these NGOs convey their message and reach a wide audience. Media coverage of police and governmental harassment of the NGOs aroused public anger and disapproval, winning support for the opposition. Second, news coverage often helped NGOs to recruit new volunteers. As people became aware of prodemocracy NGOs, more citizens came forward to join. In interviews with Strategic Marketing Media Institute, Optor activists confirmed that news coverage helped to swell their ranks. Media coverage also boosted the morale of the staff and volunteers of these organizations, who were mostly young and politically inexperienced.

Vigilant media coverage was crucial to preventing election fraud. In the absence of an instant relay of vote counting in precincts, there was a distinct possibility that the government might have succeeded in manipulating the results. CeSid had instituted a system of parallel vote counting in each precinct. Its volunteers called or sent faxes to the Belgrade Media Center, giving the total vote counts in each location. As a result, by 10 P.M. the media center reported confidently that opposition candidate Kostunica had won the election. B92's satellite service immediately relayed the results to ANEM radio stations across the country. The results were also on the websites of CeSid, B92, and the media center. In Belgrade, Radio Index, the local municipal station, broadcast the results (B92 at that point had been taken over by the government). The election results were announced on TV Pancevo, located in a suburb of Belgrade, much to the annoyance of the Milosevic regime.

As a result, by early the next day most citizens had learned that Kostunica had won the elections, receiving 56.8 percent of the vote. Milosevic received only 34.2 percent. This prompt reporting made it extremely difficult for the regime-controlled Central Election Commission to claim victory for Milosevic. The facts of the election had gotten out too quickly for the regime to respond. The only alternative was to insist that Kostunica had failed to secure an absolute majority and therefore a second round of elections was necessary. Even this claim failed to convince a skeptical public, resulting in street demonstrations and strikes that ultimately led to the fall of the regime.

Factors Affecting the Success of Media Assistance

Several factors contributed to the success of media development efforts in Serbia. A critical variable was that media assistance was an integral part of a broad strategy to promote competitive elections. Various components of the wider effort worked in close unison, mutually reinforcing each other. Independent media provided coverage to civil society organizations, and the civil society organizations in turn bought public service advertisements that brought in revenue for the media outlets. Comprehensive coverage of election news not only was beneficial to opposition political parties but also increased the audience share of various media outlets. News reporting of the campaign also imposed a degree of pressure on the political parties to work closely together despite their differences. A synergy emerged in the efforts of opposition political parties, civil society organizations, and independent media, enhancing their collective impact on public perceptions and voting behavior.

Another contributing factor was the long-term assistance that international donors had provided for a period of years to indigenous media. Many media outlets and organizations would not have been established in the absence of outside support. Others would not have survived the political repression and economic decline plaguing the country. International aid helped to significantly expand the audience of alternative media. A decade's worth of assistance meant that donors were well placed to move quickly when the 2000 elections presented an opportunity for genuine change.

Media assistance produced dramatic results in Serbia partly because a pivotal political moment had arrived, and civic activists, journalists, and diplomats sensed it. By the summer of 2000, conditions had become ripe for change. The opposition, which had always been locked in internal power struggles, at last managed to unify around a single candidate. The United States and European Union also presented a united front and acted decisively to support the opposition in every way they could. Unlike in previous years, Milosevic's own grip on power was beginning to slip. Elements within his own security apparatus and ruling circle were beginning to distance themselves from his rule. He could no longer rely on scare tactics by referring to outside enemies, because the wars that he helped ignite were now over and Serbia had decidedly failed to secure a triumphant outcome. As a result of this political ferment, the full effect of media development aid could be realized. A similar effort ten years earlier would not have reaped the same benefits, because Milosevic's hold on power had been much stronger.

Close cooperation among international donors, often a rare phenomenon, played an important role in the success of media assistance. After the 1996 municipal elections, the donor community displayed a remarkable level of coordination. At least five donor conferences were held in different European cities to forge a consensus on policy and programs at the highest level. Implementing organizations regularly met in the field and shared information and experiences. Later, international donors even developed a single grant application so that each donor had the same information. Such a high degree of consensus and cooperation contributed to more coherent and effective media assistance programs that reinforced one another. It also led to the more efficient use of public monies and international resources.

Donors refrained from interfering in the work of the media outlets, another key ingredient in the success of the development effort. The aid in no way compromised the editorial independence of the recipients. Practically all independent media outlets criticized the NATO bombing of Serbia, but they continued to receive US assistance. Such noninterference undermined the charge that nonstate media were a tool of foreign powers. Indeed, the United States tried to maintain a low profile in Serbia and channeled its assistance through two nongovernmental organizations—IREX and Internews (which later changed its name to Invision). The delivery of aid through these NGOs proved to be a prudent course, because it was easier for media outlets to receive assistance from them than from the US government itself.

Above all, it was the commitment and vision of the journalists and managers at these independent media outlets that made the media assistance so effective. They took enormous risks in voicing their opinion for democracy and human rights. Veran Matic, director of Radio B92, later discussed how international aid complemented a domestic yearning for democracy. In an interview published in 2001, he admitted that

> at the moment when strong determination that something definitely must be done emerged inside the country, serious determination to help it from outside also emerged. However . . . no money would have been able to help us had it not been for our faith and our conviction to fight and endure. (Collin 2001, 211)

Post-Milosevic Developments

After the defeat of Milosevic and the emergence of a more open political climate, donors could pursue a more comprehensive strategy for promoting independent media. They devised new projects aimed at improving the quality of individual outlets and the legal environment for media.

Freed from having to focus exclusively on countering state repression, donors started paying more attention to professional standards of journalism. In the past, most donors had been more concerned about an outlet's political independence or opposition to the regime than editorial quality or fairness in news coverage. Conditions changed when the opposition came to power. Some media outlets remained too friendly with the new government to provide impartial, informed coverage. Even the media that had been close to the Milosevic regime sought to curry favor with the new political leadership. Donors responded to these developments by holding workshops and meetings on professional norms and ethics. Some donors encouraged local journalists to develop a voluntary code of conduct, and extensive journalism training programs were launched with the cooperation of local media institutions. IREX provided grants to the Belgrade Media Center to monitor the media and share its findings. Despite these efforts, standards of reporting and presentation remain flawed. As a recent report noted, "significant progress remains to be made in journalism quality and professional standards, but the situation was not disastrous" (IREX 2002, 209). There is a growing awareness among journalists and media firms about the need to improve standards and to institutionalize professional norms and practices, which augurs well for the future.

Donors have launched initiatives to reform the legal and regulatory framework for media. Through IREX, the US law firm Covington and Burling offered its services to the Belgrade Media Center and ANEM to help provide advice on media law. IREX also provided legal expertise to conferences and workshops on media law reform and funded the ANEM legal network that analyzes proposed media legislation and helps broadcast stations with legal work. Other donors also provided grants for the training of lawyers specializing in media law and regulation. In addition, the international community has provided funds to local journalists and media firms to participate in regional meetings on legal and regulatory issues.

Though the country has made progress on legal reform, much remains to be done. The repressive Public Information Act instituted by the Milosevic regime was repealed in February 2000, but no further reforms have been initiated (IREX 2002, 209). The constitutional right of freedom of speech has not been translated into full legal protection for free speech. Many old libel laws still remain in place and can be used to stifle journalistic inquiry.

International donors also have started focusing on prospects of economic sustainability. In the aftermath of the Milosevic regime, the United States and other donors developed training and technical assistance programs to promote their commercial viability. To cultivate marketing strategies for media, donors funded workshops and training seminars. Such efforts have had limited success at best. Most media outlets are still not run as sound business enterprises. Often, revenues through sales and advertising are insufficient to meet expenses. Independent media compete for the same limited advertising market. The problem of economic viability cannot be solved simply by upgrading management and professional skills. The country's media market is too small to support the large number of media outlets that currently exist. Unless numerous media firms are closed down or consolidated, broadcasters and publications will continue to operate in a precarious state, looking to taxpayers, vested political and economic interests, or international aid for their survival.

The Serbian experience provides valuable lessons about the nature of media assistance, out of which three points can be briefly mentioned here.

First, the proper and prudent course for international actors is to help and nurture independent media outlets without trying to influence their editorial policies. Outside interference undermines the credibility of the recipient organizations, which are likely to be viewed by the public as agents of foreign powers rather than authentic voices.

Second, although economic viability should always form part of the criteria for media assistance, donors have to remain realistic and flexible in authoritarian environments. Serbia's depressed economy was too weak to sustain a large number of profitable media firms. Moreover, corrupt, autocratic regimes tend to disrupt and distort market forces, stifling competition by intimidating advertisers associated with independent-minded media. It would have been short-sighted to have imposed strict conditions of commercial viability for recipients of aid in Serbia. The donors' overriding goal was to bolster alternative sources of information and counter the nationalist state propaganda. Encouraging economic sustainability was a secondary consideration, and rightly so. In the post-Milosevic era, it has naturally taken on more importance for donors, as media freedom is no longer in serious jeopardy. Many of the independent media outlets that emerged during Milosevic's rule will not manage to survive without outside assistance. Donors will have to choose a select few for continued support and otherwise step back and allow the media market to evolve and consolidate.

Third, recent developments in Serbia point to an underlying truth: the media largely reflect the mood and temper of a population. In recent years, Serbia has seen a shift in public attitudes and perceptions. In the 2003 elections, ultranationalist parties staged a remarkable comeback. Some independent media outlets that had crusaded for democracy and peace a few years earlier began to voice their support to chauvinistic elements. This does not render previous media assistance a failure, and international donors should not be surprised at this turn of events. In elections in 2004, a moderate liberal, Boris Tadic of the Democratic Party, defeated an ultranationalist candidate. Serbia continues to evolve toward a more democratic future, and a maturing independent media are playing a crucial role in that journey.

Notes

1. Quoted in McClear, McClear, and Graves 2003.
2. See, for example, Carothers 2001; McClear, McClear, and Graves 2003; and Sell 2002.
3. As described by Louis Sell (2002), a retired foreign service officer with years of experience in the Balkans.

4. Much of the information in this section is derived from McClear, McClear, and Graves 2003.

5. For an interesting account of B92, see Collin 2001.

6. "'B92 wasn't a reflection of the times, it was an exception,' says early listener Slobodan Brkic. 'The whole political and social climate in those days, when Milosevic was coming to power, was really conservative. B92 was a reaction to that; it was a window to the outside world, while the dominant trends in Serbia were seclusion, going back to old tribes, old values, a demagogical approach'" (Collin 2001, 26–27).

7. See, for example, McClear, McClear, and Graves 2002, 102–103, which lists many newspapers and periodicals that received grants from USAID.

8. USAID supported an IREX grant of $753,000, and OTI provided thirteen emergency grants during this period; McClear, McClear, and Graves 2002.

6

Building the Open Broadcast Network in Bosnia-Herzegovina

At the signing of the Dayton Agreement in 1995, the international community was faced with three ethnically structured, separate media systems with inflammatory reporting on other ethnic groups in each system. Nationalist parties had extensive control over the content of each of these media systems; there was little, if any, separation between politics and media. Members of the international community considered this destabilizing for the peace process in both the long and short-term. Faced with such media environment, the international community set up media restructuring as a key component of its strategy.

—L. Kendall Palmer[1]

In the winter of 1996, a few months after a tenuous peace for Bosnia-Herzegovina was negotiated in Dayton, Ohio, governments sponsoring the agreement met in Brussels to discuss the state of the country's media. After careful deliberations, they decided to establish a commercial, multiethnic television network that could provide balanced and comprehensive coverage for the whole of the country. This chapter focuses on that project, known as the Open Broadcast Network (OBN), which despite massive international assistance failed to fulfill the high expectations attached to it. The OBN case illustrates the challenges that the international community encounters in postconflict settings, including competing international agendas, anemic market conditions, weak central authority, and neglect of indigenous talent. The project also provides valuable lessons for future media development efforts.

Conflict and the Dayton Peace Accord

For the generation preceding the conflict, Bosnia was a truly multi-national society with three large religious communities living in peaceful coexistence. According to the 1991 census, Bosnian Muslims, or Bosniacs, constituted 44 percent of the population; Orthodox Christian Serbs, 31 percent; and Roman Catholic Croats, 17 percent (Thompson 1999, 209). Other smaller communities, including Jews and ethnic Turks, were also present. The three main communities speak the same language and more or less come from the same European, Slavic racial heritage. Society had become secularized, particularly in the cities, and interethnic marriages were quite common. Although not as economically prosperous as many other parts of Yugoslavia, the republic was an industrialized society with manufacturing, mining, technology, and service industries.

Bosnia had undergone a brutal ethnic conflict during World War II that left behind a degree of hostility and mutual suspicion, especially in the countryside. Croat Ustashi, allied with the Nazi puppet regime ruling Croatia, conducted a massive assault on Serbs. Two resistance forces fought the German-Italian occupation of Yugoslavia: the communist partisans, led by Josip Broz Tito, and the Serbian royalists, who favored a restoration of the Yugoslav monarchy. The two insurgencies fought each other and at times cynically exploited local ethnic rivalries. Bosnia's Serbs and Bosniacs clashed in some areas as well. More Yugoslavs died in the civil war than in fighting between resistance forces and the German Nazi occupiers. Yet the civil war did not play out strictly along ethnic lines, as members of each community fought on different sides. Afterward, myth tended to influence how the conflict was remembered and passed on to younger generations.

President Tito managed to suppress ethnic tensions from the war with remarkable political acumen and an iron hand, establishing a pluralistic society in which ethnic, confessional rivalries became dormant. Following his death in 1980, Yugoslavia started to disintegrate amid a rise in Serb nationalism. Threatening Bosnia's social consensus of tolerance, political parties were founded along ethnic lines; the Party of Democratic Action (SDA), led by Alija Izetbegovic, a Bosniac who had written about a society based on Islam; the Serbian Democratic Party (SDS), led by Radovan Karadzic, an ultranationalist advocate of a "Greater Serbia" who answered to his patrons in Serbia; and the Croatian Democratic Union (HDZ), which owed its allegiance to Franjo Tudjman in Zagreb and sought ethnic segregation.

In Bosnia's first multiparty elections in 1991, three nationalist parties captured 84 percent of the parliamentary seats. These parties had no concrete program for socioeconomic reconstruction and failed to show the kind of statesmanship that could have prevented bloodshed. Bullying tactics by the autocratic president of Serbia, Slobodan Milosevic, sparked fears that smaller ethnic communities would be stifled and dominated by the Serbs throughout Yugoslavia. The SDA was committed to total independence of the republic and with the cooperation of the HDZ voted for organizing a national referendum in 1992. The Serbian minority remained apprehensive about an independent Bosnia and wanted to remain under Belgrade's rule. With war raging in neighboring Croatia (following that republic's secession from the Yugoslav Federation) and Milosevic's army shelling Croat towns and villages, the SDS campaigned for a boycott of the referendum. But the combined votes of the Bosniac and Croat communities ensured that the referendum passed overwhelmingly.

When the republic proclaimed its independence, the Serb-led Yugoslav army and Serb militias seized control of towns in the east and north, where large Serb communities resided. The move ensured a strategic, contiguous geographic link with the Serbian republic and was meant to create the foundation for a Greater Serbia. Within a month, Belgrade-backed Serb forces managed to control almost two-thirds of the country. Serb forces also tried and failed to capture the multiethnic capital Sarajevo and instead used tanks and artillery to maintain a siege of the city, cutting off electricity, water, and food supplies. Serb forces systematically expelled and persecuted non-Serb populations in areas under their control in what came to be known as "ethnic cleansing." Notorious detention camps were set up, and killings and atrocities were employed to terrorize ethnic minorities. Women were frequently raped to terrorize and humiliate non-Serb ethnic groups. To a much lesser degree and on a much smaller scale, Croat and Bosniac forces persecuted ethnic minorities and committed atrocities as well. In spring 1993, conflict erupted between Bosnian Croat forces and the Bosniac-led Bosnian army. A US-brokered agreement ended the fighting in 1994 and led to the creation of a Muslim-Croat Federation. Political tensions persisted, however, and Croat leaders sponsored by Zagreb favored attaching Croat-populated areas to neighboring Croatia instead of remaining in an independent Bosnia.

The United States played a pivotal role in brokering a peace agreement among the warring parties in November 1995 at Wright-Patterson Air Force Base in Dayton, Ohio. The agreement was signed a month later in Paris. The Dayton accord divided the country into two administrative regions—the Federation of Bosnia and Herzegovina, and the Republika Srpska (Serbian republic). The federation was composed of territory where mainly Bosniacs and Croats now lived; the Republika Srpska covered Serb-controlled territory purged of its Bosniac and Croat communities. The agreement retained Bosnia and Herzegovina's international boundaries, established a single currency, and called for a multiethnic democratic representative government. Each entity had its own parliament, army, and police with only a tenuous link to a small, central government. The arrangement looked more like a loose confederation, and this consistently complicated the media development and reconstruction effort.

Despite the sordid role that the state- and ethnic-controlled media played before and during the conflict, the peace agreement carried no substantial provisions for establishing a free and independent media. (There was, admittedly, a brief reference to the importance of press freedom in relation to planned elections.) The agreement also failed to address the future of the divided state broadcasting system. However, the signatories did commit themselves to the "prevention and prompt suppression of any written or verbal incitement, through media or otherwise, of ethnic or religious hostility or hatred" (Thompson and De Luce 2002, 205). The responsibility for ensuring these provisions was first left to the Organization for Security and Cooperation in Europe (OSCE) and later to the Office of the High Representative.

At the time of the Dayton peace agreement, a large number of media outlets were operating in Bosnia. In 1996, Bosnia had 92 radio stations, 29 television stations, 145 news publications, and 6 news agencies (Thompson 1999, 262). Most, if not all, were under the firm control of the three nationalist parties and their allies. For example, the SDS managed Serb Radio and Television (SRT) in Republika Srpska, the SDA controlled RTV in Sarajevo, and the HDZ controlled Croatian Radio and Television (HRT) in Croat-controlled areas. The same was also true of the nonstate media. Practically all media catered to monoethnic audiences.

The war decimated the republic's once-thriving journalistic community, which had begun to blossom as communist restrictions faded in the late 1980s. Some journalists fled or were killed. Many others sacrificed their professional integrity. Most media outlets tailored their reporting and commentary to suit the nationalist parties, engaging in subtle and not-so-subtle propaganda, with scant regard to the norms of a free and fair press. Serb and Croat media outlets were usually "skeptical and often contemptuous" toward key obligations in the peace agreement concerning the return of refugees, free and fair elections, or the International Criminal Tribunal for former Yugoslavia in The Hague (Thompson 1999, 262). Bosniac media were only slightly less critical of these provisions, though still quite partisan. Only a few broadcast and print media outlets fully supported the international peace process and political pluralism. Self-censorship was pervasive, and journalists had little or no incentive to conform to professional norms. Yet there were many inducements for playing a subservient role to the dominant ethnic group in the region.

Establishing the Open Broadcast Network

It was under these conditions that the concept of an independent, commercial television network was conceived by the international community to achieve both short- and long-term objectives. The immediate objective of the network was to promote an environment in which free and fair elections, as envisaged in the Dayton accord, could be held by September 1996. These elections were deemed essential to grant the new political entity a degree of legitimacy. The international community was concerned that the existing media, largely controlled and influenced by the three ethnic political parties, would continue to feed ethnic tensions and agitate for territorial division. Donor governments hoped that the Open Broadcast Network would provide balanced news coverage, counter the effects of nationalist media, and ensure a free and fair election.

The long-term goal of the OBN project was to help develop an independent media sector. The shortcomings of the Dayton agreement, which provided for weak central institutions and left nationalist power in place, provided a strong justification for the project. Having failed to persuade the warring parties to embrace civic principles or central institutions in the peace agreement, donor governments sought to create a national network that would overcome the ethnic divide. The network would not only provide an alternative to the existing media but also demonstrate to journalists and the public what an independent broadcasting network should look like.

The US Department of State, through its Support for Eastern European Democracy (SEED) program, and European donors pledged funding and equipment to put the network on the air. The United States invested approximately $2 million during the first year and more than $1 million annually between the fiscal years 1997 and 2000. Combined with pledges from the European Commission (EC), United Kingdom, Germany, Japan, Sweden, Canada, Luxembourg, Ireland, and the Czech Republic, OBN was promised $10.2 million in funds and equipment for the first year alone. The total estimated cost of the project ranges from $15 million to $20 million.

There were two competing visions for the network. Many international donor agencies wanted to assist existing television stations and then build up an affiliate network to connect them. The approach emphasized indigenous development, building from grassroots. Others wanted to establish a "new network with journalists covering all sides of the ethnic conflict, as well as a large number of staff and officers brought from the outside" (Price 2000). OBN incorporated the elements of both visions in an incoherent way.

From the outset, in-fighting and power struggles between different international actors plagued the project. Two major international organizations—the Office of the High Representative (OHR) and the Organization for Security and Cooperation in Europe, which was charged with overseeing elections—wanted to lead the network. The international community sided with the OHR, which was entrusted with the overall responsibility for managing OBN. Initially the project was supervised by a council of donors, but in 1999, the supervisory "council" was replaced by a "board of directors, consisting of the representatives of NGOs, media industry and other groups" (De Luce 2002).

The OHR announced the project in April 1996 and established a charitable trust, the Open Broadcast Network (OBN), to receive donations and eventually turn over the assets to a local company. Named TV International Network (TVIN), it was composed of five existing stations in the federation entity. Apart from these stations in Sarajevo, Tuzla, Zenica, and Mostar, organizers planned new production studios in the Serb-majority entity, Republika Srpska, and in predominantly Croat areas in western Herzegovina. International donors assigned the International Federation of Journalists, a Brussels-based NGO, the task of drawing up a charter of editorial principles and assisting the OHR in managing donations. A governing council of donors, chaired by the OHR, was also established to oversee the network, and the OHR formed a management and editorial team.

The international bureaucrats who planned and supervised the network had no background in commercial broadcasting. Again and again they found themselves in unfamiliar territory, making mistakes that ultimately doomed the station. The first international manager of OBN had no experience in managing production and editorial operations at a commercial network. Other managers were not much better. Until 1998, OBN had difficulty registering as a business under Bosnian law and had only been allowed to operate under a memorandum agreed between the OHR, donor governments, and Bosnian authorities.

The Muslim nationalist Party of Democratic Action (SDA) saw the network as a threat to its political dominance in Bosniac-majority areas and impeded its implementation. The most vivid illustration of its opposition was the problem it created in housing the network. After the OHR selected a building in Sarajevo and paid for its refurbishing, city authorities—allied with the SDA—locked the entrance, saying that the property could not be legally rented. The OHR eventually found another location but lost valuable time. The SDA also resisted giving OBN access to a broadcasting frequency. Only after the intervention by a US presidential envoy did OBN obtain the necessary access.

Several other factors contributed to the late launch of OBN. Disagreements persisted among the international donors. Funds promised by the European Commission failed to arrive promptly and sometimes never arrived, creating resentment among the Bosnian staff and disrupting business plans. The country's mountainous geography posed a technical headache. A cumbersome satellite uplink system was employed to link the stations' transmitters. Local authorities succeeded in blocking access to some vital transmitter sites that could have enhanced OBN's reach. The undermining of OBN resembled nationalist obstruction in other key areas of the peace agreement, with Serb and Croat authorities blocking the return of refugees and virtually paralyzing the central government.

The network went on air on September 7, 1996, one week before the elections. Even then, "chaos reigned. No important editorial decisions had been made, no permanent staff had been hired at the central studio in Sarajevo, no budget had been approved and very few people had been paid. In the words of one observer, TVIN had recreated the old Yugoslav system of self-management: no one had formal authority, no one was in charge and no one had any money" (Montgomery 1997). The first evening's program consisted of a three-hour show of "amateurish news reporting and a Tina Turner concert" (Reuters, September 8, 1996). OBN could not secure affiliates in the Republika Srpska and in Croat areas because of nationalistic sentiments. As a result, the network's credibility as a service for all ethnic communities suffered. Critics saw it simply as a Bosniac operation. In 1996 the network's signal reached only 50 percent of Bosnia territory. In any case, the delay in launching OBN meant that it had little or no impact on the elections and thus failed to achieve its short-term objective.

In its haste to launch the project before the elections, the OHR paid scant attention to expenditure. Unnecessary equipment often was imported at huge cost. OBN employees were paid salaries that were two or three times higher than the prevailing rates. Affiliate stations received whatever they requested without a standard assessment of their needs. Many journalists and media owners became resentful that instead of helping worthy indigenous media entities, the international community was wasting precious resources on OBN. Even the former name of the network (TVIN) conveyed the foreign nature of the project. Instead of finding a Serbo-Croat name that Bosnians could easily identify with, the network merely retained its English-language moniker. That small example seemed to symbolize a larger, underlying problem: that donor governments were neglecting the needs of the Bosnian audience.

The poor management and rapid turnover also tarnished the image of the network. Skepticism about OBN among Sarajevo journalists was fed by a spree of firing and hiring at OBN headquarters that damaged morale and reinforced the network's reputation as an international imposition. The OHR often complained that it could not find qualified broadcast managers capable of running the network, but the problem was that talented journalists viewed OBN as a problematic newsroom. Radio Free Europe and other international media organizations had no difficulty recruiting talented editors and producers who displayed the highest professional standards (De Luce 2003). News magazine articles described the OHR staff and international managers as incompetent. Even OBN's staff joined in the criticism.[2] The critical attitude of the local media community toward the network had far-reaching consequences that the OHR and international backers failed to grasp. As the representatives of foreign embassies and international NGOs did not understand Serbo-Croat, they formed judgments about OBN not by watching its programs but by consulting Sarajevo journalists or other Bosnians.

The Open Broadcast Network also faced difficulties in obtaining assistance from outside public broadcasters. The European Broadcasting Union (EBU), a Brussels-based association that promotes the interests of public broadcasters, refused to help OBN and saw it as a commercial predator that threatened the state broadcaster in Sarajevo. The EBU had worked with pro-SDA Radio Television BiH during the war and sympathized with the latter organization's complaints about "unfair" competition from OBN. Its concerns about an internationally subsidized commercial network were later echoed by some European embassies and the EC.

OBN's inauspicious debut, high cost, and persistent ridicule from Sarajevo journalists left many donor governments uneasy. After the 1996 elections, some donors doubted the wisdom of the whole enterprise. The Netherlands, which had earlier financially supported OBN, withdrew from the project. The Open Society Institute (OSI) also disassociated itself from OBN because, in its view, the project had strayed from the original concept of empowering local stations and was dominated by international managers. Given its reputation among diplomats as the best-informed NGO operating in the Balkans, OSI's departure was particularly damaging. But the United States and the OHR were adamant in their commitment and insisted that the network needed time to take root and gain an audience.

Progress and Setbacks

After the elections, the OHR and international donors took several steps to improve the operations and programming of OBN. They hired US television consultants and sought to impose some organizational coherence on the network. They persuaded the affiliates to agree to a central hub that would produce news and set out program direction, with advertising revenues to be divided up equally. The model was supposed to resemble US affiliate networks, but the concept proved difficult to carry out.

In September 1998, OBN appointed a new executive officer and promoted a Bosnian to the post of the general manager. The management delegated more authority to the Bosnian staff and encouraged better in-house production. Managers from Western public broadcasters joined the network's governing board, adding appropriate expertise that had been sorely lacking among the donor government diplomats. OBN also took steps to improve its programming. It started showing US and European entertainment serials and films to help attract an audience to its news and current affairs programs. It hired talented journalists to improve the quality of news coverage and reporting. Consequently, its reporting and editorial quality improved. Its live talk shows were more free-wheeling than the programs on state channels. The network's evening news program, *TV INFO*, gained some respectability among impartial observers. OBN also expanded its signal to reach 70 to 80 percent of Bosnia by the end of 1998. An additional eleven stations joined the network. With a more open atmosphere in Banja Luka, a new station, Alternativa Televizija (ATV), joined the network. The addition of ATV gave OBN a genuine presence in Republika Srpska and higher quality, locally produced programming. OBN's audience ratings, however, remained disappointing and far below that of the state broadcasters. In 1999, only 12 percent of Bosniacs, and fewer Croats and Serbs, said they relied on OBN as their main source of news (US Department of State 1999).

In spring 1998, the OHR terminated the services of a highly respected Bosnian journalist, Konstantin Jovanovic. The office defended the move as a necessary shake-up of the network's staff, but it was another public relations disaster. Bosnian journalists portrayed OHR officers as neocolonialists running roughshod over talented journalists who had endured nationalist threats and pressures in wartime. The criticism reinforced SDA attacks on OBN as a foreign entity imposed on Bosnians. It was an impression the OBN failed to overcome.

A poor image among Bosnians was not the only problem that OBN faced. It also lacked realistic prospects for becoming a viable economic enterprise. Advertising revenue could not meet the cost of operating expenses. Ultimately, donors grew tired of annual funding appeals and skeptical of assurances about imminent profitability. In 1999 a consultant prepared a five-year business blueprint to make the station self-sufficient. The plan, which was adopted by the OBN governing body with some modifications, required a 20 percent reduction in dependency on donations every year for five years (1999 to 2004). Advertising, program sales, and other commercial activity were supposed to make up the difference and allow the network to thrive without receiving large injections of cash every year. Perhaps the biggest weakness of the plan, as with previous business plans, was that it assumed Bosnia's weak economy could generate sufficient advertising interest to support the costs of a network devoted mainly to current affairs programming.

Under these circumstances, both international priorities and personnel started moving away from OBN. The new high representative who assumed office at the end of 1999 did not share the enthusiasm of his predecessor. New personnel at the EC mission and other European embassies also became skeptical about the success of the network. The OHR and the EC started focusing more on reforming the state broadcasters into a genuine public service network than on keeping OBN alive. Some donors shifted funds to provide funding for changes at the newly named federation television in Sarajevo. Consequently, OBN was left with little international financial and moral support.

Ending International Support for OBN

In early 2000, the European Commission ordered an audit of OBN because the network had been slow to produce receipts. In the meantime, the EC suspended further assistance to the project. Many observers thought the audit was merely used by the EC as a means of abandoning the project. (De Luce 2002). Although the audit did not find any evidence of impropriety, it suggested that OBN lacked thorough financial controls, a criticism that could have been leveled at other recipients of media assistance. Consequently, the EC pulled out of the OBN project and by the end of 2000 refused to fund it. Once it became clear the EC would not provide further funds and even deliver some overdue payments, the United States concluded it could not foot the entire cost of the network. OBN died as an international project.

The Office of the High Representative tried to salvage OBN by proposing that the network provide programming for a newly created, countrywide public broadcasting service. The executive officer of OBN also proposed similar transition plans that would allow OBN to serve the public broadcasting stations. Bosnian staff at OBN and the journalistic community also supported such proposals. But the OBN board rejected them, fearing that the state broadcasting bureaucracy would merely strip OBN of its assets and equipment while asserting control over the programming content. Since international funding was pulled in 2000, OBN has managed to remain on the air, much to the surprise of donor governments. The network slashed expenses, laid off much of the staff, and gave up its extensive news and current affairs programming. It no longer serves as competition, journalistically or otherwise, for the state broadcasters. A private station in Croatia reportedly owns OBN.

Start of a New Television Network

After disassociating itself from OBN, the US Agency for International Development examined the feasibility of establishing a new network that would entail more local initiative and a more modest funding commitment. After careful examination, USAID decided to support Mreza Plus, which it hoped would be a more successful version of OBN, without the high price tag, multilateral infighting and foreign micro-management. The network was launched in the fall of 2001. Five of Bosnia's most commercially successful private television stations, including some former affiliates of OBN, have joined it and have agreed to share the costs of programming and marketing campaigns. In contrast to OBN, the network is managed entirely by Bosnian stations without full-time international managers. It received a $450,000 donation from USAID in 2001, $350,000 in 2002, and $140,000 in 2003, as well as $70,000 to $100,000 worth of equipment. USAID has also provided assistance ($1 million covering three years) both to strengthen local programming capacity and to produce television programs, some of which will be aired on Mreza Plus. Local production capacity has been sorely lacking in Bosnia, and the assistance will fulfill a long-felt need.

Although the network attracted a solid audience from the outset and portrayed itself as a potential direct competitor to state channels, it did not broadcast a major news program or current affairs show. Mreza Plus has yet to make a serious effort at providing news to the whole country. As a result, US assistance has practically subsidized entertainment programs and an entirely commercial enterprise. In 2003, the stations in the network did begin presenting a brief late-night newscast that airs at 11 P.M.

Many European experts question the wisdom of launching a new commercial network. According to them, the emphasis on a large, commercial network is misplaced. What the country needs most is the transformation of the existing public-sector broadcasting system by improving the quality and depth of its news programs. According to this argument, a commercial network, which devotes most of its time to entertainment and sports events, can hardly contribute to the consolidation of peace and democracy. In its haste to launch Mreza Plus, these critics argue, USAID has forgotten the overriding goals and objectives of media assistance: to nurture journalistic inquiry and viable news organizations. At the heart of this controversy are the ideological differences between European and US donor agencies.

Whereas many European donors assign an important role to public-sector broadcasting, USAID and the State Department see vibrant commercial broadcasting enterprises as the best way forward. Only time will tell whether the investment in Mreza Plus was justified.

Overall Contributions

Despite its failure as a commercial entity, the Open Broadcast Network has made significant contributions to the broadcasting sector. It opened the airwaves to activists, academics, writers, musicians, artists, and political figures who rejected nationalist ideology and who had been shut out by nationalist media. Although its journalism was often just as passive and bland as the state networks, it enabled civic voices to find their way back to the public arena. OBN arranged live televised debates between presidential candidates for the 1998 elections, the first such event in Bosnia's history. Without OBN, multi-ethnic ideas could only be found in newspapers and journals with small audiences. As one writer observed, "OBN shattered nationalist taboos, making it more difficult to spread outright falsehoods about events in other ethnic communities. Perhaps one of OBN's finest moments came during NATO's air war against Serbia in 1999" (De Luce 2002). During that conflict, the network provided a wealth of information from numerous sources in a professional, sober manner, without provocative editorial commentary, obvious bias, or blatant omission. The contrast to the nationalist media's coverage was dramatic.

OBN also injected an element of competition in the broadcast sector, acting as a catalyst for improving programming and news coverage. The inefficient, complacent state channels were forced to examine their news programming and compete for advertisers. Nationalist influence has steadily declined at the public channels. In January 2003, the federation channel broadcast a news report about a clandestine training camp run by Iranian intelligence agents during the Bosnian war. Activists from the SDA threatened and harassed journalists from the station, and police had to be posted outside the station's building for several days. Such an episode would have been unimaginable not long ago, and OBN played a role in raising the quality and integrity of the country's broadcast journalism.

The Open Broadcast Network also outpaced the state broadcasters in its public service programming, with news, educational, and documentary programs comprising 42.5 percent of its overall output (only a portion of that was locally produced, however). Only 30 percent of Republika Sprska TV's content was devoted to public service programming, as was just 34 percent of programming at Radio Television BiH in Sarajevo. In hindsight, some of OBN's harshest critics now praise it for playing a constructive role. For example, Senad Avdic, editor in chief of Slobodna Bosna, said in an interview, "OBN in its first years of operation contributed to the opening of inter-entity dialogue and helped pull down barriers between nations" (De Luce 2002). The International Crisis Group, which had harshly criticized OBN initially, later called it a "highly influential" medium. I personally have met with many observers of the Bosnian media scene who stressed OBN's positive contributions to democracy. In their view, OBN broke new ground by offering a platform for a tolerant multiethnic dialogue, thereby weakening the monopoly of the nationalist broadcasters. Thus the international investment in OBN was not a total waste.

Lessons for Future Media Assistance

The Open Broadcast Network was a well-intentioned, bold concept devised to address the pernicious propaganda of nationalist parties. The international community expected it to undermine the legitimacy of the ruling nationalists' parties, bolstering support for a more moderate, tolerant political leadership. That expectation turned out to be overly optimistic. Although it never gained an audience close to that enjoyed by the state channels, OBN undermined the monopoly of state broadcasting stations and set in motion a reform of the broadcast sector that is still under way. The OBN experiment, carried out in a difficult postwar setting with competing international interests, offers some lessons for media assistance efforts elsewhere.

The first and probably most obvious lesson is that a "top-down" approach to independent media building managed by an international bureaucracy is doomed. Instead of lending support to Bosnian entrepreneurs and journalists, the OBN project was designed and implemented by international officials and contractors. This approach proved to be OBN's greatest failing. Elaborate efforts were eventually undertaken by donors to rectify the problem, but the damage had been done. Once OBN was perceived as a foreign endeavor, managed and directed by international bureaucrats, Bosnian journalists and managers who might have joined the growth of the network were reluctant to participate.

Another equally important lesson is that the international community should pay particular attention to the management of complex media organizations it seeks to establish in a war-torn society. OBN was managed in an ad-hoc manner by diplomats, press officers, and others who lacked both experience and expertise. They failed to delineate clear responsibilities and obligations of the staff, institute strict fiscal and management controls, and adhere to deadlines. Its poor performance frustrated the donors and antagonized the local community. Had OBN hired a contracting organization or consortium with experience in the setting up and managing of a commercial broadcast organization, the outcome might have been different.

Still another important lesson is the paramount need to focus on economic viability when launching a commercial media enterprise. While planning OBN, donors and OHR did not examine the economic sustainability of the project. OBN managers failed to consider possible sources of revenues. Nor did they try to control wasteful expenditure. In fact, OBN represented a prohibitively expensive approach to countering the influence and reach of the chauvinistic media. It involved building a transmission network in daunting circumstances. The high recurring costs of OBN made it almost impossible to meet its expenditure through advertisements in such a weak economy.

The OBN experience also indicates that the international community needs to establish mechanisms to protect its investment from future misuse. After international funding was withdrawn, a Bosnian Serb businessman with ties to indicted Serb war criminals and the nationalist leadership came close to buying OBN. The episode illustrates the vulnerabilities of new media outlets in transitional societies. International donors will need to come up with policies that help protect their investment in media assistance, ensuring that equipment and other aid does not get hijacked by new owners with antidemocratic political aims.

Finally, the OBN experiment represents a warning against unrealistic expectations accompanying media assistance. OBN reflected an expectation that a commercial broadcasting network would significantly contribute to political pluralism and interethnic understanding. It was conceived and implemented against the backdrop of ethnic segregation enforced by violence and a peace agreement that sustained separate ethnic armies, police forces, schools, and parliamentary blocs.

In retrospect, the international donors placed too much faith in the potential of a commercial network to serve as a kind of magic bullet for improving Bosnia's poisoned political climate.

Notes

1. Palmer 2001.

2. For example, Konstantin Jovanovic, a prominent television journalist who worked for OBN, told a newspaper that "never in my life have I seen a project start off so badly prepared as this one. There is no information of any kind, no agency bulletins, we don't have a radio. Nothing's been done, nothing's been brought, nothing's been set up, and they are saying that we have spent some 10 million dollars already" (Thompson 1999, 287).

7

Supporting Independent Radio Stations in Indonesia

The media have been the principal means of keeping Indonesians abreast of the significant political and economic changes that have occurred since the fall of Soeharto. Media coverage has begun to make economic policymaking and corporate affairs, notoriously opaque during the Soeharto era, somewhat more transparent. Media scrutiny has also increased—at least somewhat—the potential risks for those engaged in corruption and other abuses of power.
—David G. Timberman,
Promoting Independent, Sustainable Media in Developing and Transitional Countries: The Case of Indonesia

Inexpensive and widely accessible, radio is undoubtedly the most popular medium for delivering news and information in the developing world. By describing a radio project in Indonesia, this chapter illustrates how international assistance can bolster a radio sector. After the fall of the Suharto government in 1998, USAID supported an ambitious program to improve independent radio news coverage by strengthening the skills and organizational capacities of radio stations. The program, which was designed and implemented by Internews, represents one of the largest efforts to promote independent radio in

This chapter is based on an assessment of USAID assistance to Radio Sector in Indonesia that Shanthi Kalathil and I undertook. I acknowledge her contribution herewith.

a transitional society. This chapter looks at the nature and focus of the program, its achievements and limitations, and its overall contribution to the radio sector.

Democratic Transition and the Media

Indonesia, home to 210 million people, is a predominantly Muslim country. An archipelago that spans over 3,000 miles, Indonesia features an ethnically and linguistically diverse population. The brand of Islam practiced in Indonesia is relatively pluralistic and incorporates traditional Javanese beliefs.

For over three decades, Indonesia's government was an authoritarian political regime. Under President Suharto's New Order, which lasted from 1966 to 1998, economic development took priority over building democratic institutions. Government critics were dealt with harshly, and freedom of expression was curtailed. Networks between the state, the military, and the Suharto family cronies dominated political activity.

The media environment under Suharto was characterized by strict regulations, corruption, and the prevalence of self-censorship. To promote the idea of a cohesive nation, the government restricted coverage of issues relating to ethnicity, religion, race, and intergroup issues. State-owned entities dominated the national broadcasting sector. The government required publications to obtain licenses and frequently used the licensing system to reward Suharto family cronies. Within the media sector, the relatively lively print sector displayed the most willingness to challenge government control, although broadcasters typically avoided political controversy. The government relaxed media controls slightly in the early 1990s, but tightened them again when it banned three major publications in 1994 (Timberman 2003).

By the early 1990s, the regime's authority and legitimacy had eroded significantly. The rising middle classes, Islamic groups, and dissident political leaders began demanding openness and transparency in the government. In 1998, Indonesia was rocked by a region-wide currency devaluation that severely affected the value of its currency. The resulting anger fueled massive popular protests. These protests, along with the loss of elite and military support, led to the fall of the Suharto regime. Vice President B. J. Habibie succeeded him and presided over the country's initial steps toward democracy by introducing a wide variety of political reforms.

After Suharto's fall in 1998, Indonesia's media climate began to improve. The government abolished official censorship, granted licenses to more than 1,500 new publications, and opened up the airwaves to independent news. It also eliminated state control over journalists' associations. With these reforms, media outlets expanded vigorously into different areas of news production. The broadcasting sector was liberalized, with private stations growing in size, audience, and influence. Radio stations began producing their own news programs, an unprecedented development. The parliament adopted a new press law, significantly easing restrictions on the media. Press watchdog groups were established, and overt physical intimidation of journalists declined.

In 1998 USAID decided to support independent media in Indonesia as an important element of democratic development. It commissioned a special study to review the media sector and make recommendations for future programming. The study team spent two months in Indonesia interviewing media specialists, Indonesian and foreign experts, and owners of media outlets in eleven cities on five islands. The assessment focused on television, radio, and the Internet, paying particular attention to noncommercial broadcasters (Reen and Johnson 1998, 1). The study team recommended that USAID focus on supporting independent radio stations.

Indonesia has had a long tradition of small privately owned and community-focused radio stations. Starting with the Dutch colonial period and continuing through the New Order, these stations focused on locally relevant cultural programming. After Suharto's reign ended, in 1998, the industry grew by more than 30 percent in less than two years. By 2000 the country had 750 licensed commercial stations as well as a large number of unlicensed community stations, in addition to fifty-two state-owned Radio Republik Indonesia (RRI) stations and 146 stations operated by regional and local governments (Timberman 2003). The study team gave many reasons for supporting radio. It offered a low-cost way to provide local, relevant news to communities, particularly those in remote areas neglected by newspapers and television. Radio also served as an effective medium to improve the accountability of local and national government. The study team found that local radio stations were receptive to the idea of outside assistance that would improve their news reporting and coverage.

USAID accepted the recommendations of the study team and selected Internews, which had conducted the study, to pursue the project. Initially, USAID provided a grant of US$3.38 million in April

1999 for Internews to undertake a radio assistance program as well as to promote media-based conflict resolution activities. This was followed by a $3.79 million cooperative agreement with Internews from October 2000 to March 2003. In April 2003, USAID entered into another twenty-month, $1.74 million cooperative agreement with Internews for a project focusing on building election-related media capacity. For the period spanning 1998 to 2004, Internews received about $9.18 million from USAID (including funding for the initial study).

Assistance to Radio Stations

Internews initially identified fifty initial partner stations, two from each province, to receive major assistance. They were selected on the basis of a number of criteria: the stations' willingness to establish newsrooms, their willingness to broadcast local news, their commitment to hiring and developing news staff, and their readiness to develop sustainable funding sources. Over the course of the program, additional stations also received programming assistance.

Journalism Training

During the Suharto era, radio stations were not allowed to produce their own news reports and had to rebroadcast official news from RRI, the state-owned broadcaster. As a result, when the sector opened up after 1998, radio stations were unprepared to produce independent reports and relied mainly on poorly trained, understaffed, and badly equipped news departments.

Internews sought to improve the professional capabilities of participating radio stations by providing different types of training. General training seminars delivered both basic and advanced training. Less-experienced journalists received instruction in such fundamental subjects as basic reporting and broadcasting skills and journalism theory. Senior journalists received advanced training, focusing on professional skills such as directing staff and managing resources, managing news teams, effective scheduling, and story selection.

In addition, the program trained journalists for interactive radio programming, such as quizzes and radio phone-in shows. Participants learned how to encourage audience debate, how to maintain objectivity and balance, how to handle divisive issues responsibly, and how to promote programs to increase audience participation. This specialized training encouraged radio stations to try out new types of programming.

According to Internews, only 10 to 20 percent of radio stations broadcast live programs before undergoing training; this percentage increased to 60 percent after training (Sharpe, Reen, and Allen 2003, 10).

Internews also held more specialized training programs. For example, it developed a training module specifically for conflict reporting. Called "Reporting for Peace," the program was designed to explain the role of journalists in reducing tensions in conflict situations without compromising their professional integrity. The training particularly stressed the importance of balanced and unbiased reporting and the need for countering false rumors. Indonesian journalists from conflict regions such as Aceh and East Timor participated in the Reporting for Peace program.

Internews also provided in-house consultancies to encourage the application of knowledge acquired during journalists' training. Such consultancies also gave station managers, journalists, and other staff a chance to work through problems together in a cooperative manner. Topics discussed included targeting news for specific audiences, protocols for news gathering, newsroom organization, structuring the news day, and identification of audience-specific stories and angles.

The program also organized two seminars for the training of trainers. The purpose of these seminars was to prepare journalist instructors to teach their colleagues, consult with media organizations, or teach courses on broadcast journalism. Seminars taught editors and journalists how to conduct their own training, whether in the context of their own stations or through separate organizations. The participants were encouraged to collect their own information from different sources and develop their own training material.

In addition to its own training activities, Internews worked in partnership with Indonesian organizations for training and professional development. Internews cooperated with AJI-Jakarta (Indonesian Journalists Alliance) to hold elections-related training seminars in seven cities around Indonesia. During April 2003 to November 2004, Internews undertook media training to improve the coverage of Indonesia's 2004 parliamentary and presidential elections. It stressed the importance to media outlets of maintaining independence and impartiality, as well as creative ways for journalists to engage listeners on election topics.

Generally, radio journalists who had participated in a variety of training courses compared Internews favorably to other training organizations. Many stated that the Internews sessions were better organized and more responsive to local needs. Participants also said they benefited from the international perspective provided by former BBC reporters serving as Internews trainers. The in-house consultancies proved useful to most participants in their day-to-day operations. Radio hosts and anchors used techniques learned in training to make call-in shows more lively and balanced.

However, the journalism training program was not without problems. In the beginning, expatriate trainers were not fully conversant with the conditions of the Indonesian media sector and thus were unable to provide specific advice. As a staff worker at one Jakarta station reflected, "There was a gap between participants from different parts of Indonesia and the expatriate trainer."[1] This situation improved as Internews decreased its reliance on expatriate instructors and built a cadre of Indonesian trainers. There were also problems in the participant selection process. The program sometimes failed to recruit participants who were suitable for training. Sales and marketing staff sometimes attended seminars specifically designed to instruct journalists. In addition, nonjournalists with connections to radio station owners were on occasion able to attend training seminars. This diluted the overall value of training for the radio sector.

There was some duplication in training efforts. Although Internews was the first organization to provide systematic professional radio journalism training, other international and local foundations, such as UNESCO, Germany's Friedrich Naumann Foundation, Jakarta's Institute for the Study of the Free Flow of Information (ISAI), and Radio 68H based in Indonesia, began conducting similar courses after 1998. Lack of coordination and communication between Internews and other organizations at times led to wasteful overlap and redundant efforts.

Finally, Internews encountered some difficulties in cooperating with local media organizations. Many Indonesian media NGOs resented Internews because it had received the bulk of USAID funding. Though Internews did implement some programs with local media-related civil society organizations, such as its election-related training conducted with AJI-Jakarta, its limited relationship with the local civil society hampered its effectiveness. Better communication with these civil society groups might have reduced duplication of effort in training programs. Eventually, Internews became aware of the problem and took steps to improve relations.

Management, Sales, and Marketing

Like other small business enterprises, radio stations in Indonesia tend to be owned by individuals and families. Most of them are still unprofessionally managed and may face difficulties in achieving profitability.

Because media outlets that are financially self-sufficient are typically better able to achieve editorial independence, the USAID program also focused on improving the stations' economic viability, reducing costs and strengthening revenue streams.

Internews organized management seminars in which trainers encouraged managers to develop clear organizational structures with efficient division of labor. In sales and marketing seminars, trainers emphasized the need to build sales teams and work in concert with station management and program staff. They also explained creative ideas for seeking sponsors for the news programs.

Internews provided in-house marketing and sales training, as well as in-house management consultancies, to select stations. These in-house seminars were modeled on business consulting practices and were designed to help management think through their problems and devise original solutions to them. During the second phase of the program (2000–2003), 105 participants from partner radio stations attended management/sales and marketing seminars (Sharpe, Reen, and Allen 2003).

Many of the radio station managers and business staff interviewed by the assessment team attested to the value of the management and sales training, specifically highlighting the importance of maintaining divisions between news and advertising staff. Although a few participants indicated that the management and marketing training was insufficiently tailored to individual skill levels, the majority said the overall training had been helpful. Empirical data supports these assertions. Before training, only ten of the fifty partner stations had efficient organizational structures, establishing clear lines of authority and separating individual responsibilities and duties. By 2003, forty of the stations did. Initially only fifteen stations had a general manager, program director, and sales manager, each with clearly defined roles and responsibilities. By the end of 2003, all radio stations established these positions. Audience research was previously limited to nine stations. By 2003, twenty stations were conducting audience research, and fifteen more planned to do so as soon as their financial conditions permitted (Sharpe, Reen, and Allen 2003).

Many participants interviewed by the assessment team found sales and marketing seminars particularly useful, as they provided new ideas and approaches to the participants. Stations have since started seeking sponsors for their news programs. Moreover, many stations have established sales teams. As a result of the training, most general managers have a better understanding of sales, marketing, and promotion techniques. Most partner stations now have a more balanced income stream, with 50 percent coming from national advertising and the other 50 percent derived from local advertisers and sponsors. Some radio stations reported increased revenues, which they attributed to their participation in the Internews training seminars. Not all of these changes can be attributed to instruction provided by the Internews program. Several other factors have also contributed to positive developments. During the past decade, as a result of the growth of business education and increased contacts with the outside world, small business owners—and radio station owners as a subset of this group— have acquired a better understanding of modern management practices and marketing. Indonesia's economy has also been steadily improving since Suharto's overthrow, creating new opportunities for radio stations to obtain sponsorship.

Public Affairs Programming

The Internews program also contributed to radio journalism by producing public affairs news features that ran on partner stations throughout Indonesia. Beginning in October 2000, Internews produced and distributed three weekly radio news features from its radio production unit in Jakarta. The features focused on health, the environment, and current affairs. They covered topics such as HIV AIDS, the Earth Summit, regional political issues, and the 2004 elections. Internews distributed features on compact discs via courier to all stations that had agreed to play them, at a particularly scheduled time each week. It encouraged these stations to model their own investigative reports on the weekly features and to use the features to launch local discussions. It also sponsored individually tailored, two-week internships for reporters from regional radio stations at its Jakarta production facilities, to facilitate learning about long-format programs.

The weekly features served as positive examples of professionally produced, investigative radio features, and they generally proved popular with radio stations. Internews started with 100 radio stations in twenty-five provinces, but the total soon grew to 155 stations. Internews estimated the total audience for these programs to be around fifty million per week throughout the country. For Indonesian radio listeners, the features represented some of the best investigative radio news reporting on the air. However, though the programs were informative for listeners, they generally did not inspire local stations to produce similar in-depth radio news features. Because Internews provided the programs free to its partners, stations had little incentive to pursue such programming on their own. Many also lacked the news capacity or financial resources to launch similar features.

Some stations found that the features failed to provide the local news that listeners wanted. Internews expected the features to become lead-ins for local station programming, such as talk shows and call-ins; however, in practice few stations used them in this fashion. In addition, there appeared to be no plan to sustain the weekly program once donor funding ran out.

Institutional Support

Institutional support generally took the form of limited equipment provision, Internet access, and technical training to the fifty partner stations. The technical and information technology capacities of most of the partner radio stations, especially those outside Java, were limited before receiving Internews assistance. They lacked digital recording and editing equipment, essential software, and access to the Internet. To address this problem, Internews provided Marantz and Minidisc recorders, computers, and Cool Edit Pro digital editing software to the stations. During the first phase of the program ending in 2000, Internews distributed the following equipment and software:

- 49 digital sound editing suites (DSE) computer systems
- 55 Marantz field recorders
- 50 Internet connectivity packages, including 15 ICC computers
- studio equipment and setup for Radio Jurnal Perempuan

Technical training residencies helped stations address issues such as equipment maintenance and troubleshooting, Internet use, and incorporation of digital technology. Internews also provided a phone hotline and Internet support for radio technicians and users of the digital editing software. The hotline proved to be extremely useful in the beginning. Initially it received five to ten queries every day, but once the stations became familiar with the equipment its use declined.

The provision of institutional support in the form of equipment and training improved the quality of production in addition to saving stations time and resources. For example, prior to this assistance, most partner stations transferred their news programs from the newsroom to the studio for broadcast via cassette. Afterward, most news production became fully automated, improving sound quality.

Internews also provided Internet connectivity grants to partner stations. These grants covered the cost of Internet access for a limited time, after which the stations could choose to continue or discontinue the access. The underlying expectation was that once the stations started using the Internet, they would realize that it was a powerful tool to access information and improve news and business operations. This assumption appeared justified: all fifty stations continued their Internet subscriptions once the grant ended.

Overall, institutional support enabled stations to initiate equipment modernization. Interviews and site visits by the assessment team indicated that the stations greatly benefited from the computers, software, Internet access, digital recording and editing equipment, and related support. Nearly all the stations visited during the assessment were still using the equipment provided by Internews.

Overall Contribution of Media Assistance

What has been the contribution of the assistance program to the growth of Indonesia's radio sector? At the outset, it should be recognized that this is an extremely difficult question to answer. Indonesia is large and diverse, and Internews's assistance reached only a small proportion of commercial stations. The core partners of the project represented less than 7 percent (50 out of roughly 750) of the country's radio stations. Moreover, many other factors, such as democratization, economic growth, and the rise of Islamic fundamentalism, have affected the media landscape. The effects of media assistance programs cannot be totally separated from these factors. Above all, there is no hard data from which to posit reliable conclusions. Still, a few general conclusions can be drawn.

Upgraded Professional Skills and Expertise

There is a broad consensus among the media owners, journalists, and other experts interviewed by the assessment team that the Internews media assistance program improved professional expertise in the radio sector. As mentioned earlier, the program trained radio professionals in different fields—journalism, management, sales and advertising, information technology, and even equipment maintenance. Table 7.1 shows the number of radio professionals trained each year by the program.

Table 7.1 collates the total number of participants in Internews's various courses and in-house training programs each year. Because

Table 7.1 Number of Participants in Indonesia's Internews Program, 1998–2003

1998–1999	923
2001	473
2002	507
2003	139
Total	2,042

the same individuals often attended different training activities, particularly in the journalism category, the actual number is probably smaller. Even so, the number of radio employees who received training in different fields is significant. The participants interviewed by the assessment team all attested to the value of the training in improving their skills.

There is no hard data on the utilization of skills and techniques taught in journalism training seminars and in-house consultancies. Interviews with radio stations paint a complex picture. Although most journalists were able to use some of the skills and knowledge they had acquired, several factors affected the nature and extent of utilization. The attitude of station managers was one major factor. Some stations were more willing than others to provide resources and editorial freedom to their journalists. Some stations changed their focus from news to entertainment, a development over which Internews had no control but that nonetheless detracted from the value of journalism training. Many owners of radio stations chose to submit to political influences instead of upholding journalistic principles.

The program seems to have some positive, though indirect, effects on the media sector. For example, Internews training made even non-partner stations aware of the need to improve staff skills and capacities. Some of them specifically sought Internews's assistance for this purpose. In a few cases, they hired or tried to hire away the trained staff of the partner radio stations. Some trainees became independent consultants to radio stations, contributing to the diffusion of new skills and expertise. Thus the program contributed to the growth of a small cadre of radio professionals who started spreading new ideas and practices throughout the industry.

Internews also helped diffuse, if not institutionalize, two important innovations in media training in Indonesia. First, the program emphasized practical skills that could be put to immediate use by participants. Media education in Indonesia prior to Internews's involvement tended to be highly theoretical and conducted in university classrooms rather than focused on real media environments. Second, Internews emphasized the link between financial self-sufficiency and editorial independence, providing not just journalism training but business-focused education, such as sales, advertising, and fiscal management. Some respondents indicated that as a result of the program, media organizations as well as educational institutions have started paying more attention to both practical training and commercial viability.

On balance, the program's overall contribution to upgrading professional skills in the radio subsector has been limited. The major constraining factor was Internews's decision to undertake most of the training activities itself, rather than partnering with—and nurturing—an existing local media education organization. Some critics have argued (not without justification) that had Internews worked in collaboration with an indigenous organization, it would have left a more lasting, productive legacy. The strengthened media organization might also have been able to independently attract local and international funding. Another limiting factor was the emphasis on relatively short-term training for large numbers of participants. Though many people received basic training, a much smaller proportion received the type of sustained, intensive instruction that frequently provides the most long-term benefits.

Expanded and Improved News Coverage

The Internews program devoted most of its resources to expanding news coverage by partner radio stations. The underlying assumption was that once the stations benefited from training, much-needed equipment, and technical assistance, they would expand and improve their news operations. Existing data vindicates this premise, as most of the partner radio stations have expanded their news programs as a result of the Internews project.

Prior to their participation in the program, only five out of the fifty stations (10 percent) issued news bulletins at regular intervals. The remaining stations either did not cover the news or covered it sporadically. By the end of 2003, all participating stations had established news departments and relayed news at regular intervals (Sharpe, Reen, and Allen 2003). However, this rapid expansion of news coverage cannot be attributed solely to the Internews program. Internews initially selected only stations that were interested in developing or expanding their news coverage. Moreover, as the pace for democratization grew, so did the demand for greater news coverage, putting pressure on radio stations to increase their news content.

Many partner stations also now conduct live interactive programs in which listeners call in to talk or various panels of speakers discuss national and local issues. Although live talk shows did not originate with Internews, the program's emphasis on community participation, listener involvement, and practical training in interactive programming enabled partner stations to successfully launch such programs. Its assistance also made radio journalists and talk show hosts aware of professional norms and practices while encouraging them to engage listeners in an innovative way.

Aided Democratization

Finally, the program made a positive, though limited, contribution to Indonesia's fragile democracy by providing more news and information and by enabling citizens to participate in public debate through interactive radio. By encouraging the development of news-oriented radio programming, particularly current affairs call-in shows and other interactive features, Internews helped increase citizen interaction with local government. Many radio stations now invite local government officials to participate in talk show programs, enabling ordinary citizens to question them about matters ranging from municipal issues to election matters. Occasionally such shows can even serve as a catalyst for policy reform. One station manager in Medan explained that as a result of public controversy over high parking fees, the station hosted a call-in show with the local parking official as well as a member of parliament. Following a lively on-air discussion during which many callers expressed dissatisfaction with the fees, the official parking policy was changed and the fees were lowered. Though causality is difficult to determine, the show certainly provided a direct channel between citizens and officials and may well have galvanized official attitudes on the subject.

The public affairs radio programs produced by Internews have also contributed to public understanding of health and environmental issues and current affairs from an investigative perspective. The programming has gone beyond official pronouncements, digging for facts and offering a range of opinions that many other radio news programs fail to address.

Finally, radio outlets trained by Internews often followed through on commitments to run balanced and in-depth reporting of the 2004 elections. Elections-related training enabled radio stations to devise logistical blueprints for coverage early on, which proved helpful given the complexity of the ballots and numerous polling issues. Station managers also implemented several of the electoral coverage techniques suggested during training. These included assigning teams of reporters to specific election beats and keeping abreast of poll-related media regulations. Reporters, news directors, and managers generally anticipated many of the issues that came into play during the election and were well prepared to meet the challenge.

Factors Affecting Performance

Several factors that contributed to the outcome of the program can be briefly mentioned here. First, the Internews program was based on a systematic assessment that addressed the diverse needs of existing radio stations. It developed a comprehensive package for assisting partner radio stations, with interrelated program activities producing a mutually reinforcing synergy. Journalism training improved editorial quality, and sales and advertising seminars helped stations become solvent and remain editorially independent. The provision of computers and quality recording and editing equipment supported all these activities.

Second, the program provided training in different locations to suit the needs of participating stations. Indonesia is a vast country, and its numerous islands often contain unique cultures that differ sharply from that of the capital city, Jakarta. Rather than flying participants to Jakarta for centralized training, Internews chose a locally based seminar model that enabled trainers to address specific concerns in, for instance, Sumatra, Sulawesi, or Papua.

Third, training activities were followed by individual in-house consultancies for selected stations. On-site technical assistance ensured that new skills and knowledge were better utilized with a more intense educational approach. In addition, instructors could deliver custom-made training to fit a station's specific problems.

Fourth, the project was launched at an opportune moment. Internews launched its program as the country was undergoing dramatic political and economic change and authoritarian restrictions on the media were being lifted. After the fall of the Suharto regime, public demand for news and information surged at both the national and local level. As the Indonesian economy gradually rebounded from the

Asian economic crisis, advertising sales rose and revenues for independent radio stations increased as a result. Higher revenues in turn helped expand and improve news operations at the radio stations.

Finally, the role of USAID should be mentioned. USAID funded the program generously, and the program rarely, if ever, faced a serious shortage of resources. (Indeed, many local NGOs indicated that it suffered from a surfeit rather than shortage of funds.) USAID endeavored to allow Internews the maximum freedom to adjust program activities in light of changing conditions in the media sector. Moreover, USAID also supported many other local media initiatives that enhanced or indirectly benefited the main Internews project.

In conclusion, USAID media assistance has made a tangible difference to the Indonesian radio sector. By training journalists, cultivating management expertise, honing specialized reporting skills, supporting better media regulations, and generally advancing the cause of press freedom, it has improved news coverage as well as professional standards in the radio industry. Moreover, a consistent emphasis on local news that is relevant to local communities has helped subvert the state-restricted information flow that characterized the repressive Suharto era.

However, many challenges lie ahead. Some owners have succumbed to pressure and encouraged their journalists to slant coverage in favor of vested political or economic interests. Although local media organizations are educating journalists about the negative effects of so-called envelope journalism (bribe-taking), low wages paid to journalists tend to encourage corrupt practices. A culture of self-censorship still exists. Moreover, smaller stations are still hampered by inferior, outdated equipment and lack access to state-of-the-art recording devices.

The Indonesian project offers some valuable lessons, three of which deserve special mention. First, the Indonesian experience shows that in-house consultancies combined with general training represent the most effective approach to teaching media skills. Most participants derived maximum benefit from combining general principles with the targeted advice provided through an in-house consultancy. The in-house consultancy approach works particularly well when stations are confronting structural problems that cannot be addressed through general training. Stations that had participated in in-house training showed a more sophisticated awareness not only of basic journalism practices but also of newsroom management and personnel issues.

Second, implementing organizations must have both legitimacy and a deep understanding of local conditions. Internews is an internationally respected organization with a proven track record of supporting independent media. However, Indonesian media organizations have tended to perceive Internews as an American organization that receives large amounts of funding but accomplishes relatively little and ignores local views. Although this assessment was unfair, Internews exacerbated this perception problem by failing to establish close links with local media organizations. Consequently, the NGO missed opportunities to combine efforts and leverage the impact of the project. Even if fostering links with local civil society organizations lies outside an official mandate, implementing partners should seek to build bridges with these organizations.

Finally, radio provides a low-cost way to encourage governmental transparency and accountability. Radio has the potential to reach large numbers of people and can also be highly interactive, much more so than television or print media. In conjunction with standard news programming, call-in shows can drive home the point that political issues are of direct relevance to listeners' lives. As demonstrated in Indonesia, interactive radio shows can bring citizens' concerns directly to the attention of government officials in a moderated forum, perhaps even serving as catalysts for reform.

Note

1. Interview with staff of Smart FM, Jakarta, February 24, 2004.

8

Establishing Community Radio Stations in Afghanistan

Radio Karabagh may be a microscopic study in how to build a wide proprietary interest in one of the essential pillars of democracy, a vigorous media and a free press. As Afghanistan has prepared for its first national elections . . . small stations such as Radio Karabagh have borne much of the burden of educating the populace about the candidates, the process and importance of voting. But they are also part of a deeper construction of local identity.
— *Washington Post,* October 8, 2004

Since the collapse of the Taliban regime in 2001, the international community has sponsored a substantial media assistance effort in Afghanistan to promote political stability and a pluralistic, democratic society. Donors have funded numerous projects to improve programming at state-owned Afghanistan Radio and Television, support newspapers and periodicals, and build an institutional infrastructure for the media sector. Donors also have sponsored programs to help local entrepreneurs, NGOs, and community organizations launch new radio and some television stations. This chapter focuses on one project that established a network of community radio stations

This chapter heavily draws from an assessment of the USAID media assistance program in Afghanistan conducted by Colin Soloway and Abubaker Saddique. I am grateful for the comments and suggestions by Colin Soloway.

to air local and national current affairs programming. The nature of international assistance is examined as well as the operations and challenges faced by the newly launched radio stations. In addition, the chapter considers the prospects for the stations' survival after international assistance expires.

Examining assistance to community radio in Afghanistan carries special importance because it represents the first attempt by donor governments and organizations to establish a network of community stations in a war-torn society. Prior to Afghanistan, most international assistance in war-torn societies had gone to television and print media and not to radio stations at the grassroots level. Moreover, Afghanistan is an extremely poor agrarian society with low literacy and low per capita income. Unlike other countries covered in this book, the social and economic infrastructure of Afghanistan is extremely fragile. The media development experience in Afghanistan can provide insights about the suitability of community radio stations in other developing countries traumatized by armed conflict.

A word about the concept of community radio is necessary. Although in theory a community radio station is owned by the community and is responsive to its needs and interests, community radios tend to vary in their ownership the world over. In Afghanistan, these stations fall under two categories. Most the stations are owned and managed by individuals but are supported by the community. Such support usually comes in the form of a gift of land, building, or even voluntary time by community members. In addition, some stations are owned and managed by nongovernmental organizations. These stations were originally started by NGOs but later incorporated in Internews's network. For example, the Canadian NGO IMPACS started three women's stations: Radio Rabia-e-Balkhi in Mazar-e-Sharit, Radio Zorah in Kunduz, and Radio Sahar in Herat.

International Media Assistance

When the Taliban regime fell in 2001, the country's media was in a state of ruin. Freedom of expression had been extinguished. With its extreme, fanatical interpretation of Islam, the Taliban had instituted a highly repressive political system, banning television footage as blasphemous. The state radio network was renamed Radio Sharia and was employed for religious and political indoctrination. The radio relayed sermons, religious debates among preachers, and political tirades against the opposition. A handful of newspapers were published under strict censorship. No opposition newspapers were allowed, although some newspapers published in Pakistan found their way into the country. The Taliban virtually cut off the country from the outside world, only permitting correspondents from a few friendly countries, such as Pakistan and Saudi Arabia. Although some Afghans listened to local language broadcasts by the British Broadcasting Corporation, Voice of America, Radio Pakistan, and All India Radio, they faced severe punishment if caught. Thus, as a commentator aptly put it, Afghanistan under the Taliban was a country without news and pictures—literally. In the regions controlled by the Northern Alliance, the media situation was only marginally better. Local media dutifully toed the official line and glorified ruling warlords.

Conditions began to change quickly with the establishment of a new interim government in December 2001. Censorship was abolished. The victorious Northern Alliance swiftly took over the state-owned radio stations. With the end of the Taliban's draconian rules, radio stations started playing popular music for the first time in six years. Independent newspapers sprouted up in major cities. Foreign correspondents from around the world descended on the country, covering local and national news. Major Western powers, particularly the United States, the United Kingdom, and Germany, beefed up their information services to provide news and information and to counteract the legacy of Taliban propaganda.

The international community started promoting indigenous media to promote democracy and political stability. It provided transmitters, computers, and other equipment to the state-owned Afghanistan Radio and Television and trained its journalists and management staff. The broadcaster's operating expenses were also covered in some cases. Such assistance helped Radio Afghanistan to expand its reach and improve its operations, though its efficiency and objectivity remained in question. In addition, donor governments and organizations helped revive state-owned television, which had been shut down by the Taliban. Several international organizations also gave financial and technical assistance to emerging print media. Because of widespread illiteracy and the high cost of newsprint, the newly established publications were unable to cover their expenses through sales and advertising. Timely international assistance assured the initial survival of these fledgling newspapers and magazines.

The donor community has also tried to improve the institutional infrastructure for the media sector. It has helped in establishing local

NGOs committed to democracy and press freedom and given grants to local educational institutions to develop courses on journalism. Some donors also provided technical assistance to the government to reform the legal and regulatory environment for the media. Finally, the international community has helped local entrepreneurs, NGOs, and community organizations launch independent radio and even television stations, which are run as commercial or nonprofit enterprises. The objective is to lay the foundation of an independent broadcasting sector that is both editorially professional and commercially self-sustaining.

Since the establishment of the provisional government, the US Agency for International Development (USAID) has funded numerous media projects. It has particularly focused on radio, which is undoubtedly the most popular and easily accessible medium in Afghanistan. Like other international donors, it provided commodity and technical assistance to Afghanistan Radio and Television. It also funded Radio Arman, which has the distinction of being the country's first independent commercial station. Radio Arman, which came on air in March 2003, has been an instant success, playing Pashto, Hindi, Persian, and even Western pop music, lonely heart shows, and sport features. The agency also has supported a network of community stations to disseminate local and national news and information.

Promoting Community Stations

In February 2003 USAID signed a cooperative agreement with Internews, which was already managing many of its media initiatives, to establish fourteen radio stations across the country. Internews was to select locations and owners for the stations, loan necessary equipment, train radio staff and journalists, and take other steps necessary to ensure the stations' long-term survival and growth. Once the project ended in June 2004, it provided additional resources to establish twenty more radio stations by March 2005.

Internews explored two options. One was to develop a national network carried by repeat FM stations. The second option was to initiate a network of community stations that would enjoy autonomy over their own programming but also broadcast centrally produced content. After discussions with USAID, Internews settled on the second option for a number of reasons. First, instead of a national endeavor imported and imposed from a distant city, the project encouraged local participation and ownership; local leaders, entrepreneurs, and communities would have a stake in the management and successful operation of the radio stations. Second, community radio stations would provide an unprecedented voice and a forum for isolated villages and towns by covering local news, personal and community announcements, and other subjects. They could cultivate dialogue and discussion on important local issues. Third, the overall costs and operating expenses of community radio stations would be much less compared to integrated FM stations (Soloway and Saddique 2005).

Internews has followed three criteria to select locations for radio stations: (1) the stations should be dispersed throughout the country rather than concentrated in a single or few regions; (2) the community to be served should be large enough to support an independent station, as very small communities cannot generate enough advertising or revenue from public announcements; and (3) there should be demonstrable local support for the venture, with the local community either donating land or housing the station and pledging to pay a part of building and maintenance costs. Entrepreneurs should have at least $1,000 available for investment in the station. Internews also has screened potential managers and owners to assess their interest and business capabilities.

Each new station receives a "radio station in a box," which includes cased racks of recorders, players and amplifiers, a small mixing desk, a computer loaded with the recording software Cool Edit Pro, microphones, and portable tape recorders for reporting. In addition, it receives at minimum a 150-watt FM transmitter and, if necessary, a thirty-meter tower. Because of the chronic shortage of power, Internews sometimes provides a generator to run the station and transmitter. All equipment remains the property of Internews, which has the right to reclaim it. The total cost of the package varies depending on the needs of the station, ranging from $12,000 to $100,000. It includes $3,000 for six months of salaries for a station's director, general producer, and technical director ($150, $100, and $100 per month, respectively), and supplemental fuel and transport expenses (Soloway and Saddique 2005).

Once a community is selected, Internews invites senior staff of the planned station to Kabul for three weeks of journalism and technical training, including practical instruction on a dummy radio station. Internews also sends an expert to the station before it becomes operational. The expert helps managers and reporters install the necessary machinery and equipment, institute an organizational structure, and solve early problems. When necessary, Internews also helps in building makeshift studios with locally available material, ranging from cardboard to canvas.

In addition, Internews provides constant technical advice and assistance. It has two full-time business development specialists to help stations prepare suitable strategies for increasing its revenues, including preparing fees for advertising, paid requests, and community announcements. Since September 2004, Internews has started funding the position of an advertising/business director for each station. Selected candidates receive sales and advertising training in Kabul. Internews and other organizations also give special grants. For example, USAID gave the Killid station a powerful transmitter to boost its signal over Kabul and $170,000 for training its management and business staff.

All community stations receive radio programming produced by Internews and other organizations, which is distributed by Tanin (Echo) distribution network. Funded jointly by USAID and the European Commission, Tanin distributes as many as thirty-four separate programs, which vary from Internews's *Shahrak Atfal* (Children's City) to AINA's *Dar Velayat, Tchi Migzarad* (What's Happening in the Provinces?) to the farmer's program *Kesht-e Khob, Haasil e Khob* (Good Planting, Good Production). Making up for a lack of newspaper distribution, Solowa Tanin also delivers the most popular newspapers and magazines, from which broadcasters often read to their listeners. Tanin's packets are carried via a network of taxi drivers every day to community radio and state-owned stations.

In June 2004, the community network and a handful of state-owned radio stations started receiving *Salaam Watandar* (Hello Nation), a ninety-minute morning and evening broadcast of news and entertainment programming produced by Internews. Radio stations receive the program via standard digital television satellite decoders, and rebroadcast the show over their local transmitters. *Salaam Watandar* employs a network of local journalists around the country to report on events in their areas. Internews plans to expand the *Salaam Watandar* feed to five hours—and eventually eight hours—of daily programming. It is exploring various options so that the program can be self-sustaining.

Salaam Watandar and Tanin programming provide community stations with an essential base to build an audience. The material helps fill air time with useful, professionally produced news and current affairs features. Moreover, *Salaam Watandar* has become a steady source of income to the stations, as they receive a share of revenues from commercial and public service announcements on the program.

Progress and Performance

By the end of November 2004, twenty-five community stations had become operational. Most stations operate for limited hours, ranging from eight to twelve hours. Practically all are located in modest premises, even with makeshift arrangements. Because of an unreliable power supply most stations use electric generators, which increases operating costs. A few stations have now started employing solar panels to cut their fuel bills.

In addition to programs provided by Internews and other organizations, all stations play music from tapes and compact discs. Hindi, Pashto, Dari, and Persian music are all popular in Afghanistan. Radio stations entertain requests from listeners for songs, poetry, and other entertainment items, and usually charge a fee for such requests. Most stations have put small request boxes in selected shops; potential listeners put their requests in an envelope that is purchased from the shop for about ten cents. Such requests are a source of income to radio stations and increased customer traffic to participating shops. The *Washington Post*'s description of the letters received by the Karabagh station is typical:

> The letters that arrive at the three-room studio of Radio Karabagh are small works of folk art. They come on elaborate stationary, covered with glitter applied by hand, pictures cut from newspapers and small bits of metal foil applied like gold leaf in patterns. . . . More important for Radio Karabagh . . . are the envelopes the letters arrive in. Sold by the local merchants for the price of four Afghanis—about 10 cents—the envelopes raise revenue for the station. They contain requests for music, praise for the station and sometimes facts offered in the interest of greater general knowledge. (*Washington Post,* October 8, 2004)

Still more important are community and personal announcements. Stations announce upcoming community events, meetings, and other information either for free or for a nominal fee. Personal announcements about weddings and funerals are most popular. Such announcements save a family considerable time and effort, as otherwise they would need to roam the countryside on foot or donkey to inform their relatives and friends. The fee for such announcements ranges between 100 and 200 Afghanis (between $2 and $4).

Most radio stations also produce local news, interview community leaders, and even read interesting stories and poems from newspapers and magazines. A few stations hold discussions on important topics affecting the community. Some stations also air religious programs. Stations owned or run by women NGOs focus on health, sanitation, child rearing, cooking, literacy, and other more sensitive women's issues, such as forced marriages and domestic violence.

In Kandahar, Azad Afghan Radio acts as a watch dog and advocate on local issues such as the power supply, availability of drinking water, and the performance of the municipal administration. (Soloway and Saddique 2005). A few other stations have started relaying "people's voices" programs in which they interview ordinary people at random about their views on various topics and problems. Such interviews often highlight specific problems and even force local leaders to find solutions. For instance, in Logar province Radio Milli Paygham conducted interviews with local farmers and traders, revealing that a lack of reliable public transportation to Kabul was a major problem. They had difficulties ferrying local produce to Kabul and bringing back consumer goods. "The station's reporters embarked on an on-air odyssey from local to provincial governments to find out who was responsible for the transport situation. When they finally found the provincial minister responsible, they elicited a promise to arrange more buses for commuters to Kabul" (Soloway and Saddique 2005). Though the outcome is still unknown, the incident highlights the potential role that community radio stations can play in articulating public grievances and bringing them to the notice of local authorities.

The community stations also relay news features and public service announcements on important national issues. Such programs carry substantial educational value in a country where only 30 percent of the populace is able to read and write. Community stations played a useful role educating voters before the presidential elections held in October 2004. They provided information about candidates, polling booths, time and dates of elections, procedures for voting, and voters' rights and obligations. In many remote areas, community radios were the only source of such information. Sometimes the election campaign coverage produced instant results. For example, a promotion on Mazar's Rabia-e-Balkhi station calling for increased registration of women resulted in 500 women turning up in front of the station before going to register en masse.

The quality of programming and local reporting at the stations remains poor, which is hardly surprising given the country's recent history and the existing physical and institutional constraints. Most journalists lack both extensive training and journalism experience. Their general education tends to be lacking as well. These journalists and producers are learning on the job and have no one to guide them. It naturally will take time before community radio stations conform to the standards of professional journalism in developing societies, much less to those of more mature democracies.

Anecdotal evidence indicates that community stations have become quite popular and have succeeded in gaining a substantial audience. With the exception of Killid, all community stations visited by a USAID assessment team reported between 70 and 100 percent audience share in their local communities. This confirms anecdotal evidence that Afghans tend to prefer FM stations over shortwave and AM stations. Moreover, in small communities such as Ghoriyan, Bamiyan, and Karabagh, the stations do not face any competition except from shortwave and state-owned regional programs. Therefore an FM channel carrying local and national news and Hindi, Pashto, and popular music can attract a large audience. In relatively larger media markets such as Mazar-e-Sharit and Kabul, community stations face more intense competition.

One measure of audience involvement is the amount of listener mail flowing to the stations. Each week the stations receive 100 to 400 letters, containing community and personal announcements, song requests, and complaints about local officials or government. In Bamiyan, the station manager reported that the station also receives five or six "walk-in" visitors a day who come to read poems or make announcements (Soloway and Saddique 2005).

Journalistic Independence and Self-Censorship

Although the stations are not subject to official censorship, they seem to exercise extensive self-censorship. They are keenly aware that there are cultural, social, and political boundaries that they must not cross. For example, radio stations are circumspect in covering women's issues. Even the stations owned by women NGOs are careful not to give the impression that they question the traditional status and roles of women in Afghan society. As the director of Radio Rabia-e-Balkhi reported to the USAID assessment team, "if we acted freely for one day, our office would be closed down. We're trying to help women deal with their difficult family problems, their kids that are out of control. If we just tell her 'you know, a woman can be president,' we will be criticized, and get in trouble. And what good will that do these women?" (Soloway and Saddique 2005).

The station, which is named after a famed Afghan woman poet, has still managed to broach delicate women's issues while retaining a large audience. Devoting about 70 percent of its programming to shows catering to women's concerns, the station discusses child rearing, cooking, and hygiene and formerly taboo subjects such as forced marriages, domestic violence, divorce, and female suicide. When certain subjects are too volatile, the station sometimes raises issues indirectly through dramatic productions.

Almost all stations are reluctant to cover sensitive political topics and prominent personalities. They tend to ignore subjects such as political corruption, intimidation by warlords, the role of local elites in poppy cultivation, and the unethical practices of powerful businessmen. In interviews with a USAID assessment team, the radio stations were candid about their cautious approach. The country still suffers from the legacy of prolonged civil war and the political and economic uncertainty associated with it. Community stations have little or no protection against powerful vested interests, especially in small communities and remote areas. The consequences of exposing the privileged and the powerful could be disastrous for the survival of a station and its staff members.

However, there are cases in which a community station succeeded in taking a bold stand and remained on air. Radio Karabagh reported from listeners' letters that Kabul's mayor exploited a teachers' day ceremony to make a political speech praising the mujahideen. The mayor denied it and demanded that he review all critical letters about him before they were read on the air. When the station refused, the mayor took the case to the local council, or *shura*. The council backed the station.

Some stations play it safe by avoiding local news and events. For example, Radio Tiraj-e-Mir in Pul-e-Khumri has not expanded its programming beyond *Salaam Watandar* and popular music. As one local observer described it, "Tiraj-e-Mir is treated by the local commanders like their personal jukebox. They send their men around to make requests for their favorite songs for their boys to dance to" (Soloway and Saddique 2005). The same is true with Radio Sharq in Jalalabad. Given the deep and violent divisions between rival warlords and militia commanders and the absence of the rule of law, the station has yet to air any local news program and has primarily focused on a diverse mix of music.

Some community stations are also facing a potential problem due to their relationship with donor governments. Provincial reconstruction teams, or PRTs, are under the jurisdiction of the US Department of Defense and include military civil affairs units and USAID advisers. Many PRTs view the community radio stations as useful partners for their public affairs and psychological operations messages. They believe that because the community radios are funded by the US government, the stations should fully cooperate with them, particularly on poppy eradication and counterterrorism campaigns. Many PRTs are even willing to heavily subsidize the stations. However, a close identification of community stations with PRTs can compromise their independent status. There is the risk that Afghans may start seeing them as instruments of foreign authority rather than independent media entities. In war-torn societies such as Afghanistan, the dividing line between propaganda and news is thin indeed, and economically struggling stations may be tempted to cross it. Both USAID and Internews are aware of the challenge.

Sustainability of Community Stations

A major unanswered question is the sustainability of the community stations. Can they survive without international assistance in one form or the other? It is too early to say because community stations are an entirely new phenomenon in Afghanistan and there is little empirical evidence to make future predictions. Even so, a few general observations can be made to illuminate the issue.

Since the beginning of the program, Internews has been concerned about the financial viability of community radio stations and has taken steps to cultivate it. Internews gives preference to those proposals in which managers and local leaders demonstrate the motivation and skill to run stations as sound business enterprises. Internews emphasizes business skills in its training activities and provides technical assistance to secure advertising and sponsors. It has recently recruited experts to provide advice to interested community stations in seeking greater revenue. Internews also is exploring other possible revenue streams such as supplying stations with video satellite (VSAT) systems that can provide a feed to fee-charging Internet cafés.

All community stations raise revenues from different sources—national advertising, local advertising, announcements, and listeners' requests. National advertising revenues come through the program *Salaam Watandar.* Internews negotiates advertising contracts with commercial firms, intergovernmental organizations, and NGOs that want to get their message out on radio. It then shares advertising revenue among the participating stations on the basis of each outlet's market size. Whereas large stations in major cities currently earn between $1,000 and $1,500 per month, small stations average around $400. At present, *Salaam Watandar* is the largest source of income to community radio stations. Other revenue sources, particularly for the smaller stations, are paid requests for songs and personal announcements. As noted earlier, stations charge a few Afghanis for an envelope to be deposited in special request boxes around town. In some cases the boxes attract so much traffic that merchants are willing to pay stations to put them in their stores. No precise data are available, but for many stations such requests are the second most important source of income. Some stations have been able to earn $100 to $200 monthly from announcements and requests. Finally, stations, particularly in major cities, solicit advertising from local traders and businessmen.

Internews remains optimistic that most stations will be able to raise enough revenues to meet operating expenditure. Moreover, many more will manage with modest assistance from the international community. Although this may be true, one should not ignore the structural barriers to long-term sustainability in such a difficult setting as Afghanistan, barriers that are beyond the control of the stations or international NGOs.

The limited local market for commercial advertising represents one obvious obstacle to sustainability. Afghanistan is extremely poor, and most people depend on subsistence agriculture that generates little surplus. Although manufacturing and trading sectors are growing, most of the firms operate at such a small scale that they have little use for advertising. Consequently, many community stations find it difficult to generate significant advertising revenues. For example, Radio Nadaye Sulhe in Ghoriyan, which enjoys 100 percent of the local audience share and strong public support, has been unable to earn more than $100 a month from local advertising. Another station, Milli e Paygham in Logar province, earns only $250 a month by selling advertising to local merchants. Only the stations located in large urban areas can realistically expect significant local advertising revenues from local enterprises.

Even so, some experts believe that there is considerable untapped potential for advertising revenues in local markets. They argue that many small firms can be persuaded to advertise on radio stations, provided the rates are reasonable and the benefits of advertising visible. Exponents of this view argue that Afghani businessmen who returned from foreign countries after the fall of the Taliban are aware of modern sales and advertising practices. They are also very entrepreneurial and enterprising. So the task of obtaining advertising is not as difficult as it seems. There are already cases where enterprising radio managers have been able to tap the local market. The advertising manager of Radio Naw e Bahar in Balkh City was able to solicit commercials worth $1,500 during his first week. The manager approached small traders and farmers and succeeded. Although other stations might not be able to replicate his achievement, it does point to the potential for advertising in provincial towns.

Another potential obstacle to sustainability is that public service announcements, which are the major source of revenue to community radio stations, are likely to decline in the future. At present, most advertising revenues, which stations receive from *Salaam Watandar,* come from the advertising funded by international intergovernmental organizations, European and US NGOs, and major development agencies. However, the experience of recent postconflict societies indicates that as countries achieve political and economic stability, the volume of public service announcements declines. Gradually, the international community no longer sees the need to run media campaigns and withdraws funding for public service spots. Afghanistan is not likely to be an exception.

It also seems doubtful that *Salaam Watandar* or similar programs would be able to attract substantial commercial advertising to meet the losses incurred by declining public service announcements. Afghanistan does not have many multinational or national firms that advertise nationally. It will take at least ten to fifteen years before large firms, which allocate significant budgets to sales and advertising, emerge on the national scene. And, even if they emerge, large firms are more likely to advertise in greater urban markets than in small towns and villages, where people have little disposable income to spend on consumer goods.

The last obstacle is competition from commercial radio. As the independent media sector grows, many commercial radio stations will compete with community stations for advertising and public service spots. In fact, USAID has already given grants to a Kabul-based commercial station, Arman FM, to establish repeat stations in Afghan providences. As a result, community stations in Mazar, Herat, Ghazni, and Kandahar would have to compete with well-funded network stations that could take away audience numbers and advertising.

Under these circumstances it would be unrealistic to assume that a majority of the stations could become and remain economically viable. Some stations that are able to meet most of their operating expenses might be in trouble if *Salaam Watandar* fails to obtain the current volume of public service advertising or is no longer subsidized by USAID and other donors. At the time of the USAID assessment in October 2004, Internews reported that six out of fifteen operating community stations had become self-sufficient. A closer examination by the assessment team indicated that only three were actually functioning without any direct support from Internews or other NGOs.

The long-term survival of community stations will depend on several factors, including continued political stability in the country, economic growth in the areas where the stations operate, the entrepreneurial abilities of station directors, and the degree to which operating expenses are kept under control. Moreover, the direct and indirect technical assistance that different media NGOs and international agencies provide will also be a critical factor. Finally, the legal and regulatory framework for media that evolves in Afghanistan may shape the future health of the stations. For example, if the government provides some protection to community stations against commercial or state-owned media, these stations may have a better chance for survival.

In the meantime, many stations will require financial assistance for years to come, though the amount will be relatively small, ranging from $500 to $1,500 per month. As the stations gain experience, they will be able to manage with even less. For example, Radio Rabia-e-Balkhi receives only $550 a month ($500 from IMPACS and $50 from Internews) and has been able to survive. International donors and NGOs may be forthcoming to aid those stations that serve their communities and aggressively seek local revenues. If the international community fails to provide necessary support, many stations would have to fold.

Concluding Remarks

Internews has succeeded in establishing a network of independent community stations within a time span of two years, an extraordinary achievement given the daunting conditions. These stations broadcast the national *Salaam Watandar,* providing national and international news. They also provide useful information on a range of vital problems facing the country and educate people on public issues. Most stations also have their own local news programs, giving a voice to the local community for the first time. The stations provide useful social services, such as airing community and personal announcements. Although the quality of local programming is sometimes flawed and amateur, it is improving. Long-term economic viability remains a question, but most stations can survive for another five to seven years with modest assistance from Internews or other international organizations.

The experience of establishing community stations in Afghanistan provides three distinct but interrelated lessons. First, many media experts initially doubted the wisdom of establishing community stations in Afghanistan, favoring instead a national, centralized network. They were concerned that the local communities might fail to provide necessary support for such a project. They also were apprehensive about the provision of training and technical assistance because of poor transportation links. Some even doubted the ability of these stations to produce local programming in the absence of experienced journalists. These concerns have proved to be unjustified. Most stations are running reasonably well and are charting new territory in towns that never enjoyed the benefits of any local broadcast media. The project has demonstrated that international organizations can promote community stations in impoverished war-torn societies that have had no experience of independent or commercial media.

Second, the Afghanistan example also suggests that community radio stations can raise modest resources locally. As mentioned earlier, community radios have succeeded in earning revenues from diverse sources—local advertising, requests for songs and poems, community and personal announcements, and national programming. Although the revenues are insufficient to meet operating costs, they are significant nonetheless. The project also suggests that the staff of the newly established stations can be trained to tap these revenue sources.

Third, in a politically and economically fragile environment most community stations may require long-term financial support, though the level of aid would decline over time. It is unrealistic to assume that community stations could become economically viable within a year or two in such difficult conditions. Although some may succeed, most are unlikely to achieve such a feat. Therefore it is important that donors prepare a long-term strategy for supporting the stations. Though every effort should be made to promote economic sustainability from the outset, international donors should be prepared to offer a helping hand to the needy stations. Otherwise, the whole investment might be wasted.

9

The Talking Drum Studio in Sierra Leone

*By giving voice and visibility to all people—including and espe-
cially the poor, the marginalized and members of minorities—the
media can help remedy the inequalities, the corruption, the ethnic
tensions and human rights abuses that form the root causes of so
many conflicts.*

—Kofi Annan, UN Secretary-General[1]

This chapter describes an internationally funded media program to
promote peace and reconciliation in a postconflict society. Search for
Common Ground, an international nongovernmental organization
with headquarters in Washington, D.C., launched the Talking Drum
Studio (TDS) in Sierra Leone in 2000. The studio produces news
and entertainment programs for a general audience as well as war-
affected groups, including refugees, internally displaced persons, ex-
combatants, and children. The Talking Drum Studio distributes its
programs to participating radio stations to air at negotiated times.
Surveys indicate that the TDS programs have proved popular and
have helped to reduce social and political tensions while bolstering
the radio sector. This chapter describes the organization and philoso-
phy of TDS, the nature of its programming, and the project's contributions to Sierra Leone society. Search for Common Ground has a
sister program, the Community Peace-building Unit (CPU), which
works in close cooperation with TDS; however, that program is not
discussed here.

Political Context

Sierra Leone is a small West African country with a population of about 4.5 million. It is endowed with rich agricultural land and marine and mineral resources, particularly diamonds and iron. Although the country is home to seventeen ethnic groups, two—the Mendes and Temnes, each with a population of nearly 32 percent—predominate. This richly endowed but extremely impoverished country experienced brutal civil wars throughout the 1990s. The violent conflicts that engulfed Sierra Leone cannot be attributed to any ethnic, religious, or ideological differences among the population. Instead, armed conflict was the result of political mismanagement and exploitation by authoritarian rulers on the one hand, and the greed of powerful foreign interests for the country's diamonds on the other. The warring parties, however, shamelessly exploited ethnic identities to prolong and sustain violence.

Since securing its independence from the United Kingdom in 1961, Sierra Leone has been governed by authoritarian figures trampling individual freedom and undermining the growth of democratic institutions. Under increasing domestic pressure the ruling party, the All People's Congress, started to liberalize political life in 1991, when a rebel militia, the Revolutionary United Front (RUF), launched a civil war with the encouragement of Charles Taylor from Liberia. As the armed struggle escalated, both government and rebel forces engaged in forceful extraction of diamonds. Combatants looted private properties and terrorized civilians. Rebel forces recruited and indoctrinated young soldiers and forced them to commit atrocities against their own communities so that they could not return to their homes. These gangs of uprooted militia bands had a stake in perpetuating the conflict.

In 1996 Sierra Leone held elections resulting in the establishment of a new civilian government. The new government signed a peace accord with RUF, known as the Abidjan peace agreement, raising hopes for peace. Such hopes were shattered when the civilian government was overthrown by a military coup. The coup leaders, who professed commitment to democracy, established the Armed Forces Ruling Council (AFRC) to govern the country. The international community, particularly African countries, launched a diplomatic initiative to restore civilian rule. When all efforts failed, the Economic Community of West African States Monitoring Group (ECOMOG) requested Nigerian forces to remove the military regime in 1998. Rebel forces launched a large-scale attack on the capital in

1999, capturing its eastern and central districts. Again, ECOMOG mobilized Nigerian forces to push out the rebels and restore order in the country.

Comprehensive peace negotiations between the government and rebels, conducted under the auspices of ECOMOG, led to a peace accord, known as the Lomé peace agreement. The accord, which was signed in 1999, provided amnesty to combatants, guaranteed senior positions to rebel leaders in the government, and made provision for the demobilization and reintegration of ex-combatants. The two parties agreed that the United Nations and ECOMOG would monitor the implementation of the accord. Subsequently, the United Nations established a 17,000-strong UN peace-keeping force in Sierra Leone (UNAMSIL, the UN Mission to Sierra Leone) to maintain peace and lay the groundwork for a democratic transition. The settlement brought to an end years of civil war that claimed 15,000 lives, displaced nearly 40 percent of the country's population, and shattered its physical and institutional infrastructure.

At the time of the peace agreement, the media sector in Sierra Leone was in total disarray. Although the country had a long tradition of newspapers going back to 1801, when the *Sierra Leone Gazette* was first published, it had only a few independent newspapers in 1999 (Sesay and Hughes 2004). Most were published at irregular intervals, depending upon the availability of newsprint and other resources. The government published an official newspaper, the *Sierra News,* that reflected its policies and interests. The government also owned the country's only television station and an FM station in the capital, Freetown. Only four independent radio stations operated in the country; two in the capital, and the remaining two in provincial towns. All the independent media outlets—print and electronic—depended on the generosity of important clients, particularly international donor agencies.

Since 2000, the international community has provided assistance to strengthen the country's fragile media sector. It has donated financial and commodity support to public and private media outlets, initiated programs to train journalists, and helped media NGOs. The British Department for International Development (DFID) gave technical assistance to help the government establish a broadcasting regulatory body, the Independent Media Commission. Many international donors have assisted with the setting up of new radio stations. For example, the British Broadcasting Corporation was instrumental in establishing the Voice of the Handicapped, FM 96.4, and Voice of America helped launch KISS FM in the provincial town of Bo. The

DFID supported Radio Democracy, which moved to Freetown when the war ended. In addition, UNAMSIL established its own radio station, UNAMSIL 103.3 FM, which has its branches in provincial towns.

Organization and Approach

Search for Common Ground, which uses media to promote peace in war-torn societies, launched the Talking Drum Studio in June 2000. It structured TDS along the lines of a previous project in Burundi called Studio Ijambo. As in Burundi, the overarching objective of TDS was to support democratic development in Sierra Leone by producing radio programs that promote mutual understanding and goodwill among diverse groups. TDS also focuses on major social and economic problems that may ignite civic unrest and violent conflict. Its programs explore the settlement of refugees and internally displaced persons, reintegration of ex-combatants, the HIV/AIDS epidemic, social and political tensions, children and youth issues, and gender discrimination.

TDS's emphasis on conflict resolution makes it distinct from standard media development efforts. The project's reporting and news coverage differ from that of mainstream journalism. Indeed, its sponsors believe that "traditional journalism" usually stresses conflict and even rewards discordant behavior "with airtime and newspaper space, while efforts to build consensus and solve problems are penalized— by being either ignored or discounted" (Marks 2003, 15). TDS, in comparison, gives prominence to national and local efforts to reduce tensions. The studio's programs are designed to foster understanding among different viewpoints and highlight the shared values and interests of divergent groups, encouraging solutions to common problems.

TDS works with various civil society organizations, international agencies, and government agencies. For example, it has established collaborative relationships with the National Commission for Resettlement, Reconstruction, and Rehabilitation; the National Committee for Demobilization, Disarmament, and Reintegration; and the United Nations High Commissioner for Refugees (Search for Common Grounds 2003). TDS works closely with the different departments of the Sierra Leone government, and its programs are publicized by government-owned radio stations. The studio has also forged close relationships with the International Rescue Committee (IRC), which focuses on gender-based violence, and the USAID-funded Campaign for the Victims of Torture, which seeks to address war trauma among women, children, and youth. Such relationships have contributed to the legitimacy and effectiveness of TDS but are in sharp contrast to the established norms of independent media, which tend to keep government and other major organizations at arm's length to ensure editorial independence.

TDS produces programs that are both entertaining and informative. The project recognizes that peace-building programs need not be boring. In Sierra Leone, as in other war-torn societies, citizens are tired of speeches by political leaders, descriptions of international intensions, and the bleak picture presented by news and events. Instead they look for programs that both entertain and educate. Seeking to make programs as accessible as possible, TDS relies on soap operas, storytelling, dramas, and public discussions. These programs are usually better platforms for disseminating a message than dry reporting of news or exhortations to peace by political and social leaders.

Since its start in June 2000, TDS has expanded its production capacities and staff. It now operates three production sites, one in Freetown, and the other two in the provincial towns of Bo and Makeni. It produces seven national programs in Krio (the national dialect) and eight regional and local programs. The studio employs forty full-time and twenty-two part-time staff, including security guards, drivers, and administrative employees. In addition, the program recruits consultants and interns to conduct special studies and to advise its management and production personnel. The composition of the studio's staff is multiethnic and has a balance of men and women.

Search for Common Ground has been quite successful in attracting multidonor, multiyear funding for the project. Initially most of the funds came from USAID and the Dutch Foreign Ministry, but eventually many other donors—such as the UK's DFID, the European Commission, the Swedish International Development Cooperation Agency, the Swiss Agency for International Development and Cooperation, UN High Commissioner for Refugees (UNHCR), and the Canadian Department of Foreign Affairs—also lent support. The volume of international assistance has steadily increased, from $730,000 in 2000, to $1,675,000 in 2004 (Temple 2004, 13).

Program Production and Distribution

TDS develops programming and content, taking into consideration audience requests, suggestions by national and international organizations, and recommendations from regional and central staff. It changes its programs to reflect evolving social and political conditions. For example, as violence in Sierra Leone has subsided, TDS has shifted its focus from peace and reconciliation themes to solving major problems facing the country. It also ensures that women have an equal voice in programming decisions.

TDS has signed agreements with eighteen of the country's current twenty radio stations to air its programs. The remaining two stations did not join the TDS network because they demanded commercial rates for broadcasting the studio's programs. Although TDS does not pay commercial fees to stations for airing its programs, it does provide financial and technical assistance to the stations. The studio offers an assistance package of between of two and three million Leones (approximately $740 to $1,111) to different partner stations for a six-month period. Such assistance covers fuel and staff costs, stationery, and personnel training. TDS negotiates the amount of financial assistance with a station by taking into consideration its transmission range and hours of broadcast. It also supports stations with emergency needs—generator repairs, rent, or licensing fees— on an ad hoc basis.

In addition to financial assistance, TDS provides training and technical assistance. The training is designed to help stations improve business operations, explore innovative ways to raise funds, and manage expenses prudently. For example, in Kabala, local groups and radio Bintumani organized a dance raising eight million Leones. The station used the money to buy a Honda motorcycle for its reporters. TDS also assists stations with organizational development, focusing on topics such as establishing a board of directors, appropriate management strategies, and reporting procedures. It also provides training in conflict resolution and interview techniques to journalists employed by radio stations. TDS monitors partner stations to ensure that programs are aired at agreed schedules.

Current TDS Programs

The Talking Drum Studio currently produces seven national and eight local programs (Search for Common Ground 2003). Following are brief descriptions of these programs:

National Programs

Common Ground News Feature follows a magazine-style format, focusing on stories that represent the interests and concerns of rival groups. It provides balanced coverage of divisive issues and includes voices of supporters of RUF. News features are interspersed with peace messages, music by local musicians, and human-interest stories. The *Common Ground News Feature* airs twice a week for a half-hour on sixteen stations.

Golden Kids News is produced by children under adult supervision and provides a forum for children to discuss their hopes and fears. It engages children with different backgrounds who serve as producers, reporters, and presenters. It aims to highlight children's problems and promote advocacy groups concerned with child welfare. Golden Kids News airs twice a week for fifteen minutes on sixteen stations.

Wi Yone Salone provides information about developments all over the country by interviewing people on a wide range of current issues. It also provides information on development activities being undertaken in different districts. This twenty-eight–minute program is produced weekly and aired on sixteen radio stations.

Salon Uman covers the status and role of women in postconflict Sierra Leone. Produced with the help of local human rights groups, it identifies current developments that are affecting women. *Salon Uman* also serves as a platform to advocate for legislation to protect women's rights. Produced twice weekly, this fifteen-minute program is aired on sixteen radio stations.

Home Sweet Home focuses on refugees and internally displaced persons. It intertwines information with dialogue to provide an entertaining drama that informs and educates refugees and returnees about the problems they face on their return. The program also provides information about government policies concerning resettlement of refugees and internally displaced persons, safe areas, and other relevant topics. *Home Sweet Home* is sponsored by UNHCR and is played on sixteen radio stations twice a week for thirty minutes.

Atunda Ayenda is a soap opera about the youth of Sierra Leone, which discusses the circumstances that led them to join armed militias and the difficulties they had in leaving them. It also examines the impact of the war on people by interviewing a cross-section of the population. This radio drama is intended to develop critical thinking among young people about their problems and prospects. It is produced daily for fifteen minutes, with a thirty-minute summary on weekends, and is relayed on eleven radio stations.

Parliament Bol Hat grew out of the work of independent radio stations during the previous general elections. The program focuses on parliamentary debates and discussions, exposing the audience to how democratically established institutions operate. The program is carried by sixteen stations.

In addition to the national programs, TDS produces the following local and regional programs:

Local Programs

Leh We Tok focuses on the Bo district and provides a forum for people to voice their concerns and opinions. A thirty-minute program, it is produced in Bo and aired daily on two local radio stations.

Mu Gondehedesia is a Mende cultural program that looks at customs and traditions through stories. It aims at reviving the cultural heritage of the Mende people. A fifteen-minute program, it is produced in Bo twice a week and aired on three radio stations.

Trait Tok is a program for teenagers and by teenagers that focuses on HIV/AIDS and related sexual and social issues that affect them. This fifteen-minute program is produced twice a week and is aired on eight radio stations.

Kalimera is a Temne-language program that explores customs and traditions through stories and parables. It also focuses on opportunities for peaceful reconciliation of conflict through traditional approaches. This fifteen-minute program is produced in Makeni and is aired on three radio stations.

Maborama is a Limba cultural program featuring traditions and stories that promote social healing and cohesion. *Maborama* airs fifteen minutes per week on three radio stations.

Unity Boat is a soap opera that focuses on people in the forest region of the eastern province. It aims to foster social reintegration of refugees and internally displaced persons returning back home after many years. Produced in both the Kissi and Mende languages three times a week, it airs on three radio stations.

Sisi Aminata focuses on HIV/AIDS and is produced in cooperation with the National AIDS Secretariat. Produced each week, this fifteen-minute program educates people about HIV/AIDS and answers questions from teenagers. It also provides medical advice.

Na Yu No Mor also focuses on HIV/AIDS and is produced once a month. It seeks to explore the changing face of HIV/AIDS vis-à-vis the population of Sierra Leone.

Audience surveys indicate that most of the studio's programs are popular, reaching a cross-section of the Sierra Leone population. Sixty to 80 percent of respondents have heard about the programs, and nearly half of the respondents attempted to listen to one or more of them during the month of the interview (Abdallah, Shepler, and Hussein 2002). Interviews with informed members of the Sierra Leone media sector and civil society confirm these findings. The local and regional programs have a limited audience simply because of their reliance on local languages.

Contributions to Sierra Leone Society

Search for Common Ground and donor agencies have conducted studies and evaluations to examine the effect and the impact of the Talking Drum Studio project. (Abdallah, Shepler, and Hussein 2002; Search for Common Ground 2004f; Temple 2004; Everett, Williams, and Myers 2004). These studies and evaluations point to TDS's three contributions, which are briefly discussed here.

Providing Information and Ideas

TDS continues to disseminate useful and timely news, information, and ideas. In interviews, key informants have emphasized three features of TDS. First, its programs reach a nationwide audience, including areas that were once strongholds of rebel forces. It has successfully resisted the impulse to simply focus on the capital or important regions. Second, it covers a broad spectrum of subjects and issues, ranging from the settlement of refugees and internally displaced people to elections and HIV/AIDS. Such broad coverage has proven useful to different groups and constituencies. Third, its programming has given voice to ordinary or poor people who were previously overlooked and ignored by local media and the political leadership (Abdallah, Shepler, and Hussein 2002). The studio's interviews with common people have been a refreshing development in the country's media landscape.

Many TDS programs seek to provide practical information that can be used by the targeted audience. For example, *Home Sweet Home* informs people about government policies and programs for resettling refugees and internally displaced persons. It also raises awareness about the problems that they might face and ways to overcome them. Similarly, *Troway Di Gun* (now discontinued) informed ex-combatants about the economic and social opportunities available if they surrendered their arms. More important, it provided a forum to share concerns and problems. The radio programs on HIV/AIDS often provide practical advice to patients as well as to the public. Such information is usually not offered by conventional news programs but is crucial in a country with high rates of illiteracy.

In addition, TDS programs have improved the sensitivities of the listening public. For example, *Golden Kid News,* a popular program, has raised some awareness about children's problems and predicaments. Many informants indicated that people gained a new understanding of their children after listening to the program. *Solan Uman* has highlighted the problems of gender violence and discrimination in this male-dominated society. At least a section of women who listen to the program "are more aware of their rights, and are more vocal and protective of them" (Temple 2004, 22). *Sisi Aminata* and *Na Yu No Mor* "have managed to bring the highly sensitive HIV/AIDS epidemic to the attention of the population, particularly the youth" (Everett, Williams, and Myers 2004). TDS programs have educated and continue to educate a section of the people on a range of topics and problems.

TDS programming has occasionally sparked some civic and community action. A recent listeners' survey indicated that "almost three quarters (73%) of respondents noted some community actions that resulted from listening to TDS radio shows and participating in events" (Temple 2004, 20). For example, TDS has helped to improve relations between people and security sector officials in Makeni, where the general public tends to distrust the police and the military. Negative public perceptions, however, changed as a result of an agreement between TDS and the police and military in which all parties agreed to remove sources of mistrust and misunderstanding. Radio Mankneh launched an information campaign to improve relations between people and the police and military. The improved relations partly contributed to an early withdrawal by UNAMSIL from the region. These are isolated examples, and no generalizations should be made.

Reducing Tensions

By providing balanced news and information, some TDS programs have also helped to ease tensions, particularly between ex-combatants and the government. The demobilization and resettlement of ex-combatants provides a good example. Since the beginning of its operations, TDS earned the trust of fighting factions by reporting facts and giving combatants opportunities to articulate their grievances. It often met with officials of rebel groups and broadcast interviews. It also interviewed government officials and sought their responses to the issues raised by rebel commanders. Such interactive, balanced reporting encouraged the ongoing dialogue between the government and ex-combatants. TDS news coverage often dispelled misgivings among ex-combatants. For example, some former soldiers were concerned that once they gave up their arms, they would be incarcerated. TDS aired interviews with the disarmed soldiers, who publicly stated that such apprehensions were unjustified. Such interviews along with official assurances helped dispel misgivings, contributing to the demobilization effort.

According to a recent DFID evaluation of the TDS program, "Just about everybody interviewed, including ex-combatants from all fighting factions, believed the success of the disarmament and demobilization process was in part due to the sensitization role undertaken by TDS and information they provided about the National Committee for Disarmament and Demobilizationprogram" (Temple 2004, 19).

In many cases, TDS has also worked with its sister organization, the Community Peace-building Unit, to resolve local conflicts.[2] For instance, in Mile 91 (a town in central Sierra Leone) the chiefs and local council members quarreled over the collection and use of public revenues. When the two parties failed to reach an agreement, people brought the problem to the TDS office. TDS and CPU contacted the appropriate officials in Freetown and the concerned parties in Mile 91. TDS's partner Radio Gbafth aired its phone-in discussions with the Freetown officials to discuss individual responsibilities for tax collection. The station then organized a roundtable radio program in which the chiefs, councilors, and Freetown officials discussed the problem and clarified their respective roles and responsibilities. In this case, TDS not only reported facts but also promoted a successful dialogue.

With the active support of TDS, its partner stations occasionally launch innovative initiatives that bridge the divide among rival communities or defuse disputes. For example, Radio Moa in Kailahun has started a messaging service to help unite divided families and to allow parents to appeal to their children to stop fighting in Liberia and to return home. The station also resolved a potentially explosive issue. People in Kailahun were under the wrong impression that they were being singled out by the government to pay taxes. By airing a nationwide report explaining the tax system, who pays, and what the revenues were used for, the radio station dispelled local misgivings.

Strengthening the Radio Sector

Finally, a major but often ignored contribution of the Talking Drum Studio is that it has strengthened the radio sector. It has helped with the establishment of community radio stations in remote parts of the country. When the project started its programming, organizers realized that many parts of the country lacked adequate radio transmission equipment. Consequently, TDS worked with international donors to establish community radio stations. The European Community provided funds to establish two radio stations in the northern part of the country. Later, TDS worked with the charity World Vision International, which administered USAID funds to provide communities with the necessary radio equipment. Although TDS cannot take credit for the growth of community radio stations, it did encourage and bolster the process.

More important has been the technical and financial assistance that TDS has been providing to partner stations. The financial assistance, though modest, has been critical to many stations that cannot depend simply on advertisements and public sponsorship. Moreover, TDS training and technical assistance have helped stations improve their management and business operations. Such assistance has been particularly useful, as the country lacks experience in running stations as commercial enterprises.

TDS has also helped to spread programming skills and ideas throughout the radio industry. For example, programs such as *Mr. Spider,* broadcast by Radio Gbafth in Mile 91; *Mr. Eagle,* of Radio Mankneh in Makeni; and *Mr. Owl,* aired on Kiss FM in Bo, are based on TDS productions (Temple 2004). Though these programs are not exact replicas of TDS programs, their creators were clearly inspired by previous Talking Drum Studio efforts. This emulation illustrates how radio stations value TDS programming and confirms the project's positive influence.

Some observers have suggested that the TDS approach to news reporting and coverage is improving professional norms of radio journalism.[3] Some Sierra Leonean reporters are now presenting their stories in a less sensationalized manner and do not hesitate to report unpopular opinions. They also try to present news in more constructive ways. Although there is no hard data to substantiate such observations, this seems quite probable. The studio is a major media actor in Sierra Leone, and its programs enjoy credibility both among the government and the public. Therefore it is quite possible that the TDS journalism style has some impact on professional norms and practices.

TDS partner stations have also started "phone-in programs," especially in areas where cell phones are available. For example, in Makeni, Radio Mankneh runs a phone-in program that invites civil servants (such as government officials, teachers, and doctors) to answer public questions such as "Why are the roads deplorable?" "Why are teachers who are facing serious misconduct allegations still teaching?" "Why do rape victims have to pay for treatment?" and "What steps are being taken to improve medical facilities?" The program has drawn a large audience.

Several factors have contributed to the success of the Talking Drum Studio. It was launched just after the Lomé peace agreement was signed, at a time of genuine yearning for peace in the country. The media sector was totally devastated, and there was a nationwide demand for news and information that could reduce tensions and promote mutual understanding. Moreover, the program was well designed and well conceived. Search for Common Ground had a wealth of experience in supporting similar projects and applied that knowledge to the Sierra Leone effort.

Still another factor in the studio's success was the project's reliance on local talent. The role of expatriate staff has been limited, preventing unnecessary tension that has sometimes engulfed other international media programs. The project's expatriate staff is aware that TDS success depends on the active cooperation and participation of local staff. Regional office managers also provide important strategic direction.

The program has benefited from the generous funding of the international community. Multiyear funding of TDS by different donors has assured rational planning and execution. TDS managers did not face uncertainties about the project's survival each year and could focus on the substance of the project in a deliberate manner.

Problems and Challenges

Although there is little doubt that the Talking Drum Studio has helped in consolidating peace in Sierra Leone, one should not underestimate its problems and limitations. Temple (2004) has suggested that TDS staff members are under constant pressure and often face ambiguity about their roles and responsibilities. Their roles as members of a family, community, or tribe occasionally conflict with their professional duties. Their work sometimes puts them in an adversarial position with their family, community, and tribe, and as a result they face hostility from within their primary social groups.

The project also faces the challenge of unrealistic expectations. Because of the credibility of some of its programming, Talking Drum Studio is often expected to address far more topics than it is able given the current size of its staff. Although setting down a set of selection criteria has helped the studio to focus on specific topics, the public demands on the project are still enormous. Audience members urge the studio to cover myriad events, and local organizations seek TDS's collaboration. These audience members and organizations are naturally disappointed when TDS is unable to comply with their requests. This problem is particularly acute when the studio's limited staff has to cover large areas such as Makeni and Kono.

Some journalists question the studio's approach to news and reporting, arguing that TDS is often too friendly with government officials and international agencies. Government decrees often treat official information as secret, giving reluctant officials an excuse not to divulge unpalatable facts. As a result, the ministries can—and frequently do—withhold important information. Senior officials often treat information as a tool to promote their political and bureaucratic interests. In its quest for conflict resolution, TDS sometimes avoids challenging government officials on sensitive and controversial issues. TDS also avoids openly criticizing opposition or former rebel groups for their past and present misdeeds. According to these journalists, though TDS's nonconfrontational approach has contributed to its survival and growth, the project may have set a bad example for aspiring journalists. The TDS example fails to encourage journalists to challenge the existing power structure.

Although there is substance in such criticism, it is not fully justified. It overlooks the nature of TDS as an essentially public education endeavor launched in a war-torn society to promote peace and reconciliation. The studio does not purport to be a value-free news agency. Moreover, its nonconfrontational approach does not necessarily mean that journalists abstain from seeking facts or avoid investigative reporting. The difference between TDS and conventional journalism is sometimes more a matter of style than substance. However, it is important that it maintains its independence and does not compromise its professional integrity.

Finally, the most important question about TDS concerns its sustainability. It is entirely supported by donor agencies. It never tried to raise local resources as, according to Sierra Leone law, nongovernmental organizations cannot collect revenue from fees, sales, or advertisements. But donor agencies are unlikely to support the program indefinitely. As the country becomes more politically and economically stable, donors will probably choose to withdraw their support. Therefore an "exit strategy" is needed to retain some of the programming without undue reliance on foreign resources. Search for Common Ground is aware of this challenge and is working on it. It is yet to be seen whether the NGO will be successful in its efforts.

The experience of Talking Drum Studio illustrates a promising model for media programs to contribute to building peace in societies torn by internal conflicts. The project shows that international agencies can produce media programming that is both entertaining and educational and air that content on both public and private outlets. Instead of competing with local radio stations, the studio serves as a resource and helps the stations through technical and financial assistance in addition to donating programming. Projects such as Talking Drum Studio not only can reduce tensions and promote reconciliation by providing balanced and constructive coverage of problems in a politically fragile environment but also can strengthen a country's fledgling electronic media sector.

Notes

1. Quoted in Ross, Howard, Rolt, Van de Veen, and Verhoeven 2004, 7.
2. The CPU uses a divergent strand of approaches to achieve its aims, including supporting the establishment of community radio stations; organizing musical peace festivals, soccer tournaments, and live drama performances; and facilitating conflict resolution through community dialogue.
3. E.g., Stanley Bangura, Radio Mankneh public relations officer.

10

Recommendations to the International Community

Rather than resorting to censorship and counterpropaganda, Washington should make use of the greatest weapon it has in its arsenal: the values enshrined in the First Amendment of the US Constitution. The State Department should make the promotion of independent media a major priority in those countries where oppression breeds terrorism. . . . The State Department should therefore apply strong diplomatic pressure, including perhaps the threat of making future aid conditional on compliance, to influence governments in these countries to adopt laws and policies that promote greater media freedom.
—David Hoffman, Internews Network president[1]

The preceding chapters examined the nature, achievements, and limitations of media development projects in different countries while also identifying programmatic lessons. There is no need to recapitulate or elaborate on these lessons and the implications for media development initiatives. Consequently, this chapter outlines only a few policy recommendations for the international donor community.

Focus on Closed and Semidemocratic Regimes

Although the international community has undertaken media projects in Africa, Asia, and Latin America, most assistance has been devoted to Southeastern Europe and countries of the former Soviet Union. After the collapse of communism, such an approach was undoubtedly prudent and logical. Media assistance helped many of these countries to consolidate fledgling democracies and bolstered a fragile peace in the Balkans. However, it is important that the international community now shift its focus to other parts of the world where media assistance is badly needed. Donors should concentrate in particular on the closed and semidemocratic regimes of Africa, Central Asia, and the Middle East, where such assistance could have a tremendously positive impact.

These closed societies are ruled by monarchs, military juntas, or extremist ideologues who trample human rights and prevent broad political participation. Burma, Cuba, Iran, North Korea, Saudi Arabia, Sudan, United Arab Emirates, and Vietnam are among these closed societies. Even though extractive industries produce a high level of per capita income for some of these countries, the economies are essentially underdeveloped and dominated by central authority. Deep political tensions fester under the surface but remain dormant. These regimes stifle the flow of information and prevent the emergence of an independent media sector. The international donor community has limited programmatic options in most closed societies because the repressive regimes are suspicious of any projects seeking to establish independent, sustainable media. Still, donors can often initiate modest interventions that can lay the groundwork for democracy and an independent media.

For example, donors can support emerging civil society groups that carry the potential of eventually promoting independent media. Such groups may include associations of local journalists, intellectuals, lawyers, and writers. Moreover, donors can foster training programs to improve technical skills of print and broadcast journalists. Generally, authoritarian regimes tend not to object to such training because they are confident of their ability to exert control over the media. The international community can also provide travel grants and scholarships to local journalists so that they can observe the workings of free media abroad. During the Cold War, such travel grants and exchange visits widened the political horizons of journalists visiting from communist societies.

The opportunities for fashioning media programs in semidemocratic regimes are much greater. In such countries, though some political freedom is permitted and rudimentary democratic institutions exist, political power remains concentrated in the hands of selected groups or authoritarian rulers. Independent media remains fragile, and subtle forms of censorship and self-censorship are pervasive. The legal and regulatory environment also tends to discourage and obstruct the functioning of a free media. The majority of countries in Africa, Central Asia, and the Middle East fall under this category. Examples may include countries as diverse as Malawi, Morocco, Egypt, Ethiopia, Jordan, Kenya, Sierra Leone, Turkey, Uganda, and Zambia. Carefully planned media assistance programs can make a real difference in such settings. Depending on local circumstances, donors can offer programs on journalism, management training, legal and regulatory reform, privatization of state-owned media, and the strengthening of media organizations.

Strike a Balance in Meeting Current Needs and Building Viable Institutions

Like all development interventions, most media programs fall under two broad categories: those addressing current needs, and those focusing on long-term institution building. Training and technical assistance projects for journalists and media firms illustrate the first category. Such programs seek to solve immediate problems faced by the media sector. For example, the regional television project in Russia helped struggling stations that lacked trained journalists and business skills. Although addressing short-term requirements, such assistance does not necessarily build indigenous capacities to deal with such problems in the future. The second category involves building long-term institutional capacity. For example, international donors funded media law institutes in Russia and Indonesia, which now assist media firms, local media NGOs, and even government departments and agencies. In Russia, the institute also offers courses on media law and regulations and has trained a cadre of media lawyers.

In the past, most international media assistance was devoted to solving pressing problems facing the fragile media sector, particularly in transitional European countries. This emphasis on a short-term mindset stems from several factors. The international community was concerned that promising political openings would be missed due to any delay in delivering assistance. Moreover, donor agencies preferred programs that produced instant results to satisfy their political constituencies. Therefore, many media NGOs preferred to directly train journalists than to invest in building local institutions for instruction.

Institution building remains an uncertain and arduous process, and international donors tend to be risk averse.

The international community, however, should adjust course by giving equal, if not greater, priority to institution building. Although it should not ignore current needs, the primary goal of media assistance should be to build local capacities. Without such a long-term emphasis, the effect of worthy media development efforts can quickly fade away. The donor community may provide legal assistance to governmental and nongovernmental organizations, but its main objective should be to help law faculties in universities or independent law institutes cultivate expertise in media law and regulation. Encouragingly, there is a growing consensus among international donors about the need for strengthening institutional capacities of media-related organizations and institutions.

Give Priority to Developing Local Radio Stations

If media programs are to be expanded in closed and semidemocratic societies in the developing world, the international community will need to recognize the importance and reach of radio. Most of the transitional and war-torn societies in Europe and Eurasia that received assistance in the past were relatively advanced. Literacy rates were high, and newspapers were widely available. Communist governments had also built up a network of television stations. Yet developing societies present a much different set of conditions and challenges. Due to low literacy rates, poor transportation services, and the relatively high cost of publications, print media fails to reach a majority of the population. Most television stations are owned by the state and usually reach audiences only in urban centers. Radio remains the most popular and accessible medium, providing a link to people in distant, remote areas. Radio requires less technical infrastructure than television or print media and lower production costs. Unlike magazines, newspapers, or satellite television, radio requires no prohibitively expensive purchase price for the consumer of information. In impoverished countries, radio is the medium of the masses, touching the lives of a wide cross-section of the population.

A well-managed local radio station can be a powerful tool for promoting democracy. These stations can provide information about local as well as national and international events. The stations can also be interactive, enabling people to express their views and concerns on problems and issues that are uppermost in their minds. The two case studies of radio stations in Afghanistan and Indonesia (Chapters 7 and 8) demonstrate the positive potential of community stations and how these outlets can disseminate news and even stimulate discussions on important issues. Unlike large, national media outlets that can seem impersonal and distant, local stations often forge a direct connection to listeners in developing societies. Citizens sometimes view the stations as a kind of civic institution in which they have a stake. In the best circumstances, these stations become a genuine forum for discussion, making local governments more accountable. In addition, local stations can be instrumental in promoting economic development by disseminating market information to a wide audience of consumers and entrepreneurs. Radio stations can also spread education about agricultural innovations, micro-enterprise development, public health, and other development initiatives.

By delivering assistance to local and community radio stations, particularly in Africa, donors could have a tremendous impact on the media landscape and democratic development. Based on experience elsewhere, donors should also help build appropriate legal and regulatory frameworks for free media, impart training to managers and journalists, and, when necessary, deliver essential equipment to deserving stations. Such assistance can be channeled through governmental and nongovernmental organizations.

Exert Political Pressure on Governments

Ruling political parties, government officials, and other vested interests in closed and semidemocratic countries tend to resist major reforms in the media sector. Any progress toward independent media could undermine the regimes' tenuous hold on power. Even when regimes permit an international media project, they may put up obstacles to block the project's implementation. The international community has to recognize this reality and plan accordingly.

If experience is a guide, legal and regulatory reform is one area that will meet with stiff resistance. The international community encountered numerous obstacles in former communist countries when it sought legal and political reform. Despite their public commitments, many governments were reluctant to introduce legal reforms that would dismantle their direct or indirect control over the media. The legislative process to revise or draft new media legislation was time consuming. Moreover, the newly enacted media legislation often was not satisfactory. Even when the enacted laws were satisfactory, authorities sometimes failed to effectively carry out the amended laws. Government officials found loopholes in the legislation that violated the spirit, if not the letter, of the law. State authorities manipulated the newly established regulatory agencies and undermined procedures meant to introduce transparency. Weak judiciaries and corrupt law enforcement agencies posed yet more barriers to reform. The conditions are likely to be worse in closed and semidemocratic developing countries, where governments have no commitment to media reform and prodemocracy organizations are too weak to exert much influence.

International donors must be willing to expend political capital to pressure reluctant governments over media freedom issues. A two-pronged strategy may be required. First, donors should directly or indirectly support prodemocracy civil society organizations, which can educate and mobilize public opinion and even provide technical assistance to the government, if and when necessary. Second, they should encourage governments to create space for independent media and should not hesitate to criticize them and even impose sanctions when regimes block media freedom and pluralism.

Engage Non-Western Democracies in Media Assistance

Media assistance has tended to be led and funded primarily by the United States, Canada, and European states, or the "Western" democracies, with experts and advisers coming mainly from those societies. Yet many non-Western democracies, such as Japan, India, South Africa, Brazil, and Mexico, now have a dynamic, pluralistic media sector. They also have vibrant media and civil society organizations and well-trained media experts and teachers. Their participation would serve to strengthen the efficacy and credibility of media assistance efforts. A more diverse participation in media development would help allay the prevailing perception in developing countries that the United States and European governments are seeking to manipulate and meddle in their political systems. By making media assistance a more multinational undertaking, projects would enjoy a greater degree of legitimacy in the developing world.

Moreover, the employment of experts and consultants from non-Western countries would render assistance programs more relevant to local needs. As compared to their Western counterparts, media experts from non-Western democracies are more likely to have a deeper understanding of the media landscape of a recipient country and the challenges posed by it. A South African journalist would most likely be more able to fashion relevant journalism courses for Botswana and Lesotho than would a French journalist who has never lived in that part of the world. Similarly, the manager of a media firm from India would almost certainly be in a better position to advise media firms in Afghanistan than would a newcomer to the region from the United States. The cost of training and technical assistance also may be reduced because of the lower salaries of media consultants from non-Western democracies.

Engaging non-Western democracies in media assistance clearly carries a number of potential benefits. Even when these countries are not willing to make financial contributions, they can be persuaded to provide technical assistance or consultants.

Continue to Channel Assistance
Through International NGOs

In the past, the international community has channeled most media assistance through media NGOs. For example, USAID has used Internews, IREX, and the International Federation of Journalists for its media assistance. Such channeling of assistance has several advantages. NGOs usually enjoy greater credibility in recipient countries than private sector firms or the projects directly managed by international donors. The local political elite is generally less suspicious of the motives of these organizations. Media NGOs also provide a buffer between foreign governments and media firms and organizations in recipient countries. As assistance is channeled through NGOs, recipient organizations and media outlets are less likely to be labeled by vested interests as tools of foreign powers.

Moreover, media NGOs have accumulated considerable experience and expertise in media development work. They also have committed staff that can be easily deployed in different settings and are able to design and implement media interventions. Because of its long experience in working in war-torn societies, Internews was able to establish a network of community radio stations throughout Afghanistan within a time span of less than two years. Media NGOs also enjoy another advantage: they receive preferential treatment because of their nonprofit status. International donors usually grant them greater flexibility in managing interventions as compared to for-profit firms. Consequently, the media NGOs are usually in a better position to make suitable adjustments in their existing and planned activities when faced with a rapidly changing environment.

Media NGOs represent a suitable, proven instrument to channel assistance, and international donors should continue to work with them.

Deepen Donor Coordination

The benefits of donor cooperation in media assistance and other development endeavors are obvious but often elusive. Cooperation among international donor agencies contributes greatly to an efficient use of resources and strengthens the effect of development efforts. It avoids unnecessary duplication and prevents recipient organizations from playing one donor against another in their quest for resources. Donor agencies are also able to exercise greater influence on reluctant governments when they speak with one voice.

Yet bilateral and multilateral donors usually only seem able to work closely in war-torn societies. Each donor tends to fund its own pet programs with little regard to the priorities and plans of others. They have their own rules and requirements to allocate resources that are not always compatible with other governments or organizations. Moreover, the limited technical expertise on media assistance among some donors also inhibits the development of common strategies and programs. Small donors are often suspicious of large donors, who tend to dominate in any coordination effort. Large donors are often dismissive of suggestions coming from smaller donors. Consequently, there is some psychological resistance to donor coordination. None of these obstacles are insurmountable, however. Given political will and a shared strategy for media assistance, the situation could be improved.

At a minimum, donors should hold regular meetings and share information with each other. They should also explore new ways to secure closer coordination. Two approaches are worth mentioning here. One is the consortium model, in which different donors participate and develop a shared framework for providing assistance. Once a framework is agreed, donors can design their own projects that promote the shared goals. The international community followed this model in Serbia with tremendous success. The second model is to fund a local or regional organization, such as the Center for Latin American Journalism and the Media Institute of Southern Africa, which assumes the responsibility for developing and carrying out appropriate projects and programs. This approach can be particularly pertinent when the volume of international media assistance is limited.

Separate Media Development from Public Diplomacy

As mentioned earlier, there is a clear distinction between independent media development and public diplomacy programming. On the one hand, public diplomacy seeks to promote a country's policy interests through informing and influencing a foreign audience. Media assistance, on the other hand, seeks to enable the indigenous development of a robust, free media as a pillar of democracy. To maintain the integrity and credibility of media assistance, it is important that bilateral donors avoid employing media assistance to directly influence a foreign audience. Donors should refrain from trying to curry favor or buy the loyalty of journalists through aid programs. Nor should donors use media outlets receiving assistance to disseminate partisan propaganda. Donors entering into media development should have only one expectation—that the recipient outlets uphold standards of journalistic integrity and professionalism.

Bilateral donors can take several other measures to ensure the transparency of their efforts. One is to appoint a board of advisers composed of eminent journalists, media educators, and prominent academics or other citizens with unimpeachable reputations to advise the program. The high caliber of the advisory board can allay popular misgivings in recipient countries. Another possible measure is to leave the design and implementation responsibilities to local partners and limit the role of the intermediary organizations to general supervision and guidance. However, such a course can only be pursued when indigenous civil society organizations are capable of planning and managing media projects. Still another option for bilateral donors is to work with international organizations so that media assistance gains credibility as a multilateral—rather than bilateral—program in the host country.

* * *

In conclusion, it is difficult to overstate the significance of media freedom and an unfettered flow of information. Without it, democracy is starved, markets are stifled, and public health suffers. Cultivating and nurturing a free media has to form an integral element of any effort to build democracy. Once independent-minded news organizations find a foothold, a whole range of positive effects ripple through society and ultimately spread beyond the country's borders.

This book has attempted to illustrate how even limited media interventions can produce dramatic results in fledgling media sectors and lay the groundwork for the emergence of a genuine "Fourth Estate." Though journalists around the world face grave dangers and some societies have suffered setbacks, media freedom is steadily expanding and spreading. Media assistance has helped play a role in the growth of freedom of expression from Serbia to Sierra Leone. Developing countries in Africa and Asia have received relatively little media aid so far, and the courageous journalists and editors in those societies deserve more support and encouragement. The track record is clear, and donors can no longer ignore the potential power of media assistance. Such assistance allows taboo subjects to be discussed, makes elected officials more accountable, liberates submerged voices, defuses conflict, empowers entrepreneurs, and sometimes even helps topple despotic rulers.

Note

1. Personal communication with the author.

Bibliography

Abdallah, Amr, Susan Sheplar, and Suleiman Hussein. 2002. "Evaluation of Talking Drum Studio—Sierra Leone. Freetown, Sierra Leone: Search for Common Ground.

Alves, Rosenthal Calmon. 2002. "Challenges Democracy Created for Journalism Education in Latin America." In *Advancing Democracy through Press Freedom in the Americas*. Washington, D.C.: Inter-American Dialogue.

———. 1997. "Vanguard Newspapers in Latin America." Unpublished paper presented at the International Communication Association Conference (ICA), Montreal, Canada.

Article 19. 2002a. "Analysis of Afghanistan's 2002 Press Law." http://www.article19.org/docimages/1751.doc.

———. 2002b. "Analysis of the 2004 Law on the Mass Media." http://www.article19.org/docimages/1753.doc.

Atman, Jana. 2001. "Modest and Much Needed: Czech Media Set to Succumb to New Legislation." *Central Europe Review* 3, no. 3 (January).

Azpuru, Danorah. 2004. *Democracy Assistance to Post-Conflict Guatemala: Finding a Balance Between Details and Determinants*. The Hague, Netherlands: Clingendael.

Barya, John-Jean, Samson James Opolot, and Peter Omurangi Otim. 2004. *The Limits of No-Party Politics: The Role of International Assistance in Uganda's Democratization Process*. The Hague, Netherlands: Clingendael.

Bazala, Roz, David Cowles, Peter Graves, Dragan Kesic, Obrad Kesic, Michael Stievater, Kathryn Stratos, and Ana Trisic-Babic. 1997. "An Assessment of the Near-Term Prospects for Democratic and Economic Reform in Serbia and Montenegro." Paper prepared for US Agency for International Development, Washington, D.C.

Belgrade Media Center. 2000. "Media Monitoring Report Archives." http://www.mediacenter.org.yu/english/monitoring/monitorarhe.asp.

Belgrade Media Center and SMMRI. 2002. *Political Media Monitoring: Before and After the Change of 5th October.* Belgrade: Belgrade Media Center.

Belin, B. 1998. "Politicization and Self-Censorship in the Russian Media." http://www.rferl.org/nca/special/rmediapaper.

Bildt, Carl. 1998. *Peace Journey.* London: Weidenfeld and Nicolson.

Black, David, and David Timberman. 2001. *A Mission-wide Strategy for Enhancing the Role of the Media as a Key Actor in Indonesia's Transition.* Washington, D.C.: US Agency for International Development.

Brunner, Roland. 2002. "How to Build Public Broadcast in Post-Socialist Countries: Experience and Lessons Learned." Unpublished paper.

Carothers, Thomas. 2001. "Ousting Foreign Strongmen: Lessons from Serbia." *Carnegie Endowment for International Peace Policy Brief.* http://www.ceip.org/pubs.

Collin, Matthew. 2001. *This Is Serbia Calling: Rock 'n Roll Radio and Belgrade's Underground Resistance.* London: Serpent's Tail.

Culik, Jan. 2001. "The Death of Czech Public Service Television." *Central Europe Review* 3 (January 4). http//www.ce-review.org/.

Darbishire, Helen. 2002. "Non-Governmental Perspectives: Media Freedom Versus Information Interventions." In Monroe E. Price and Mark Thompson, eds., *Forging Peace.* Bloomington: Indiana University Press.

De Luce, Dan. 2003. *Assessment of USAID Media Assistance in Bosnia and Herzegovina 1996–2002.* Washington, D.C.: US Agency for International Development.

———. 2002. *USAID Media Assistance in Bosnia and Herzegovina.* Washington, DC: US Agency for International Development.

Development Associates. 1998. *Evaluation of the USAID Professional Media Program in Central and Eastern Europe.* Washington, D.C.: US Agency for International Development.

Everett, Paul, Tennyson Williams, and Mary Myers. 2004. "Evaluation of Search for Common Ground Activities in Sierra Leone." Unpublished report. London: DFID.

Fossato, Friana. 2001. "The Russian Media: From Popularity to Distrust." *Current History* (October): 343–348.

Frybes, Marcin. 2002. "The Transformation of the Media in Post-Communist Central Europe." In Hall Gardner, ed., *Central and Southeastern Europe in Transition: Perspectives on Success and Failure since 1989.* Westport, Conn.: Praeger.

Green, Charles H. 2002. "Latin American Journalism Center: A Case Study." Washington, D.C.: US Agency for International Development.

Gross, Peter. 2002. *Entangled Evolutions: Media and Democratization in Eastern Europe.* Washington, D.C.: Woodrow Wilson Center Press.

Harbin, Julie Poucher. 2001. "The Fall of OBN: Investigative Report." http://archiv.medienhilfe.ch/News/2001/BiH-IWPR-OBNrep.htm.

Heise, J. Arthur, and Charles H. Green. 1996. "An Unusual Approach in the United States to Latin American Journalism Education." In Richard R.

Cole, ed., *Communication in Latin America: Journalism, Mass Media, and Society.* Wilmington, Del.: Scholarly Resources.

―――. 1990. "Central American Journalism Program: Strengthening Mass Communication Education, Training, and Research in Central America." Miami: School of Journalism and Mass Communication, Florida International University.

Heise, J. Arthur, Charles H. Green, Agatha Ogazon, and the CAJP staff. 1993. *The Central American Journalism Program: An Analysis After Five Years.* Miami: School of Journalism and Mass Communication, Florida International University.

Hend, Russell H. K., ed. 2002. *Media Fortunes.* Singapore: Institute of Southeast Asian Studies.

Hoffman, David. 2002. "Beyond Public Diplomacy." *Foreign Affairs* 81, no. 2.

Holbrooke, Richard. 1998. *To End a War.* New York: Random House.

Hruby, Zdenek, Martin Cave, Chris Doyle, and Anton Marcicin. 1999. *The Economics of the Media: The Convergence of the Transition Countries with EU Member States.* Bratislava, Slovakia: Slovak Foreign Policy Association.

Hudock, Ann. 1999. *The Role of Media in Democracy: A Strategic Approach.* Washington, D.C.: Center for Democracy and Governance, US Agency for International Development.

Hume, Ellen. 2003. *Media Assistance: Best Practices and Priorities.* Washington, D.C.: US Agency for International Development.

―――. 2002. *The Media Missionaries.* Miami: John S. and James L. Knight Foundation.

Inter-American Dialogue. 2002. *Advancing Democracy through Press Freedom in the Americas.* Washington, D.C.: Inter-American Dialogue.

Internews. 2004a. "Media Monitor: The Impact of the Local Economy on Media Development." http://www.internews.org/publications/Economy_Media_Development.pdfhttp.

―――. 2004b. "Media Monitor: Women and the Media." http://www.internews.org/publications/Afghan_Media_Monitor_4.pdf.

Internews Network. 2002. "Independent Television in Russia, Grant No. 118-G-00-98-00124-00 Performance Report, June 2001–May 2002." Arcata, Calif.: Internews Network.

―――. 2001. "Independent Television in Russia, Grant No.118-G-00-98-00124-00 (August 1998–June 2001): Internews Network/Internews Russia Final Report." Arcata, Calif.: Internews Network.

Internews Network. 1998. "Independent Television in Russia: Final Report (September 1, 1995–August 31, 1998)." Arcata, Calif.: Internews Network.

Internews Russia. 2000. "Emergency Assistance to the Russian Media, Grant No. 1125 (April 1, 1999–August 31, 2000): Internews Network/Internews Russia Final Report." Moscow: Internews Russia.

IREX (International Research and Exchanges Board). 2002. "Professional Media Program, Serbia Monthly Highlights (January–July 2002)." Submitted to US Agency for International Development. Washington, D.C.: International Research and Exchanges Board.

————. 2001. "Media Sustainability Index." http://www.irex.org/msi.

————. 2000a. "Professional Media Program, Serbia and Montenegro Quarterly Report, December 31, 2000." Submitted to US Agency for International Development. Washington, D.C.: International Research and Exchanges Board.

————. 2000b. "Professional Media Program, Serbia and Montenegro Quarterly Report, March 31, 2000." Prepared for US Agency for International Development. Washington, D.C.: International Research and Exchanges Board.

————. 2000c. "Professional Media Program, Serbia Quarterly Report, July 31, 2000." Prepared for US Agency for International Development. Washington, D.C.: International Research and Exchanges Board.

————. 2000d. "Professional Media Program, Serbia Quarterly Report, October 2000." Prepared for US Agency for International Development. Washington, D.C.: International Research and Exchanges Board.

————. 1998. "Professional Media Program, Semiannual Report, July 1– December 31, 1997." Submitted to US Agency for International Development. Washington, D.C.: International Research and Exchanges Board.

————. 1997. "Professional Media Program, Semiannual Report, January 1– June 30, 1997." Submitted to US Agency for International Development. Washington. D.C.: International Research and Exchanges Board.

Janus, Noreene. 1998a. *The Latin American Journalism Project: El Salvador.* Washington, D.C.: US Agency for International Development.

————. 1998b. *The Nicaragua Program of the Latin American Journalism Project.* Washington, D.C.: US Agency for International Development.

Janus, Noreene, and Rick Rockwell. 1998. *The Latin American Journalism Project: Lessons Learned.* Washington, D.C.: US Agency for International Development.

Johnson, Eric. 1993. "Television in NIS." Unpublished paper submitted to US Agency for International Development, Washington, D.C.

Kalathil, Shanti, and Krishna Kumar. 2005. *Strengthening Independent Radio in Indonesia: An Assessment.* Washington, D.C.: US Agency for International Development.

Kimonyo, Jean Paul, Noel Twagiramungu, and Christopher Kayumba. 2004. *Supporting the Post-Genocide Transition in Rwanda: The Role of the International Community.* The Hague, Netherlands: Clingendael.

Koenig, Mark. 2002. "Draft Background Paper: Lessons Learned from USAID/Russia Independent Media Programs, 1992–2002."

Krnjevic-Miskovic, Damjan de. 2001. "Serbia's Prudent Revolution." *Journal of Democracy* 12, no. 3 (2001).

Kumar, Krishna. 2004. *USAID's Media Assistance: Policy and Programmatic Lessons.* Washington, D.C.: US Agency for International Development.

————. 2001a. "Harnessing the Media for Peace in Deeply Divided Societies: A Review of USAID's Experience." Unpublished paper.

————, ed. 2001b. *Women and Civil War: Impacts, Organizations, and Action.* Boulder: Lynne Rienner.

————, ed. 1998. *Postconflict Elections, Democratization, and International Assistance.* Boulder: Lynne Rienner.

————, ed. 1996. *Rebuilding Societies After Civil War: Critical Roles for International Assistance.* Boulder: Lynne Rienner.

Kumar, Krishna, and Laura Randall Cooper. 2003. *Promoting Independent Media in Russia: An Assessment of USAID's Media Assistance.* Washington, D.C.: US Agency for International Development.

Kurpahic, Kemal. 2003. "Prime Time Crime: Balkan Media in War and Peace." Washington, D.C.: United States Institute of Peace.

Lazar, David. 1991. "Evaluation of the Central American Journalism Project." Washington, D.C.

Marks, John. 2003. "Preface." In Howard Ross, Francis Rolt, Hans van de Veen, and Juliette Verhoeven, eds., *The Power of the Media: A Handbook for Peacebuilding.* Amsterdam: European Center for Conflict Prevention.

Maslow, Jonathan. 2002. "Nu, Chto? (What to Do?) An Evaluation of the Russian Regional Media." *Knightline International* 2: 24–29.

McClear, Rich, and Suzi McClear. 1997. *Don't Trust Anyone, Not Even Us: Yugoslav Radio Report.* Washington, D.C.: International Research and Exchanges Board and the Independent Journalism Foundation.

————. 1998. *Independent But Not Alone.* Washington, D.C.: International Research and Exchanges Board.

McClear, Rich, Suzi McClear, and Peter Graves. 2003. *US Media Assistance Programs in Serbia, July 1997–June 2002.* Washington D.C.: US Agency for International Development.

————. 2002. "I Called for Help and 100,000 People Came: Media Assistance Programs in Serbia, July 1997–June 2002. An Experience Review." Unpublished paper.

McQuail, Denis, and Karen Siune, eds. 1988. *New Media Politics: Comparative Perspectives in Western Europe.* London: Sage.

Mickiewicz, Ellen. 1995. "The Political Economy of Media Democratization." In David Stuart Lane, *Russia in Transition: Politics, Classes, and Inequalities.* White Plains, NY: Longman.

Montgomery, Michael. 1997. *A Television Station in Tumult.* London: Institute for War and Peace Reporting.

National Press Institute. 2000. *Preparing Independent Russian Media for the 21st Century: Report on Activities Undertaken Under USAID Cooperative Agreement #118-A-00-97-00274-01.* New York: Center for War, Peace, and the News Media, Department of Journalism and Mass Communication.

————. 1999. *Promoting Media Development in Post-Crisis Russia: A Report on Activities Undertaken Under USAID Cooperative Agreement #118-A-00-97-00274-01.* New York: Center for War, Peace, and the News Media, Department of Journalism and Mass Communication.

el-Nawawy, Mohammed, and Adel Iskandar. 2002. *Al-Jazeera.* Cambridge, Mass.: Westview.

Open Broadcast Network. 1999. *Report and Summary of Business Plan by Management.* Sarajevo, Bosnia: Open Broadcast Network.

Palmer, Kendall L. 2001. "Power-Sharing in Media—Integration of the Public?" http://archiv.medienhilfe.ch/News/2001/Mol-BiH0808.htm.

Peou, Sorpong. 2004. *International Assistance for Institution Building in Post-Conflict Cambodia.* The Hague, Netherlands: Clingendael.

Price, Monroe E. 2000. *Restructuring of the Media in Post-Conflict Societies: Four Perspectives.* Paper prepared for UNESCO World Press Day Conference in Geneva, May 2000.

———. 1993. "Comparing Broadcasting Structures: Transnational Perspectives and Post-Communist Examples." *Cardozo Arts and Entertainment Law Journal* 11, no. 2: 275–312.

Price, Monroe E., and Peter Krug. 2002. *The Enabling Environment for Free and Independent Media.* Washington, D.C.: US Agency for International Development.

Price, Monroe E., and Andrei Richter. 2002. *Russian Television and the Russian Public: Uneasy Transformations of Ideas of Public Service.* Oxford: Programme in Comparative Media Law and Policy Centre for Socio-Legal Studies, Oxford University.

Price, Monroe E., and Mark Thompson, eds. 2002. *Forging Peace: Intervention, Human Rights, and the Management of Media Space.* Edinburgh: University of Edinburgh Press.

Price, Monroe E., Bethany Davis Noll, and Dan De Luce. 2002. *Mapping Media Assistance.* Washington, D.C.: US Agency for International Development.

Price, Monroe E., Andrei Richter, and Peter K. Yu, eds. 2002. *Russian Media Law and Policy in the Yeltsin Decade: Essays and Documents.* The Hague, Netherlands: Kluwer Law International.

Radio Index. 1997. *The General Media Situation in Serbia.* Belgrade: Western Media.

"Radio Karabagh: The Station with Local Identification." 2004. *Washington Post,* October 8.

Rahmato, Dessalegn, and Meheret Ayenew. 2004. *Democracy Assistance to Post-Conflict Ethiopia.* The Hague, Netherlands: Clingendael.

Rantanen, Terhi. 2002. The *Global and the National: Media and Communication in Post-Communist Russia.* Lanham, Md.: Rowman and Littlefield.

Reen, Kathleen, and Eric S. Johnson. 1998. *Indonesian Broadcast Media in the Post-Suharto Period.* Washington, D.C.: US Agency for International Development.

Robinson, Raymond. 2003. "Radio as a Tool for Peace: The Studio Ijambo Experience." Unpublished paper.

Rockwell, Rick. 1998a. *Guatemalan Journalism: Advances Amidst Apathy, Fragmentation, and Manipulation.* Washington, D.C.: US Agency for International Development.

———. 1998b. *Honduran Journalism: Searching for New Boundaries, Confronting Systemic Problems.* Washington, D.C.: US Agency for International Development.

————. 1998c. *Panamanian Journalism: Pragmatic Skepticism During a Test of Democracy.* Washington, D.C.: US Agency for International Development.

Rockwell, Rick, and Noreene Janus. 2004. *Media Power in Central America.* Champaign: University of Illinois Press.

Rockwell, Rick, and Krishna Kumar. 2003. *Journalism Training and Institution Building in Central American Countries.* Washington, D.C.: US Agency for International Development.

Ross, Howard, Francis Rolt, Hans van de Veen, and Juliette Verhoeven, eds. 2003. *The Power of the Media: A Handbook for Peacebuilding.* Amsterdam: European Center for Conflict Prevention.

Rubio-Fabian, Roberto, Antonio Morales, Tomas Carbonell, Florentin Melendez, and Anne Germain Lefevre. 2004. *Democratic Transition in Post-Conflict El Salvador: The Role of International Community.* The Hague, Netherlands: Clingendael

Search for Common Ground. 2004a. *"Atunda Ayenda* as a Vehicle for Peace: Report on the Effect of the Soap Opera *Atunda Ayenda* on ex-Combatants in Postwar Sierra Leone." *Search for Common Ground* (January): 1–9.

————. 2004b. *"Atunda Ayenda:* Celebrating 500 Episodes." *Search for Common Ground* (March): 1–2.

————. 2004c. "Search for Common Ground Sierra Leone Program Overview." *Search for Common Ground* (June): 1–2.

————. 2004d. "Talking Drum Studio: Listen to Programmes Produced in and Aired Throughout Sierra Leone." September 23. http://www.talking drumstudio.org.

————. 2004e. "Talking Drum Studio Sierra Leone Listener Survey Preliminary Report." *Search for Common Ground* (August): 1–8.

————. 2004f. "Talking Drum Studio: Listener Survey Preliminary Report." Sierra Leone: Search for Common Ground.

————. 2003. "A Periodic Report on the Search for Common Ground in Sierra Leone to the British Department for International Development." Search for Common Ground (July–December): 1–18.

Sell, Louis. 2002. *Slobodan Milosevic and the Destruction of Yugoslavia.* Durham, N.C.: Duke University Press.

Sesay, Mohamed Gibril, and Charlie Hughes. 2004. *Go Beyond First Aid: Democracy Assistance to Post-Conflict Sierra Leone.* The Hague, Netherlands: Clingendael.

Shallat, Lezak. 1989. "AID and the Secret Parallel State." In Marc Edelman and Joanne Kenen, eds., *The Costa Rica Reader.* New York: Grove Weidenfeld.

Sharpe, Wayne, Kathleen Reen, and Don Allen. 2003. "Final Project Report: Strengthening Broadcast Media in Indonesia, October 1, 2000–May 31, 2003. Unpublished report. Jakarta: Internews Network.

Sigal, Ivan (in collaboration with the staffs of the Media Development Program, Internews Russia, and the National Press Institute). 1998. *Media Development Program (USAID Cooperative Agreement No. CCN-007-A-00-4136-00): Final Report.*

Sigal, Ivan (in collaboration with the staff of Internews Moscow). 1997. *A Survey of Russian Television.* Moscow: Internews Network.

Skidmore, Thomas E., and Peter H. Smith. 2001. *Modern Latin America,* fifth edition. New York: Oxford University Press.

Smajlovic, Ljiljana. 2002. *The Current Media Situation in Serbia.* Washington, D.C.: International Research and Exchanges Board. A shortened version is available online at http://www.irex.org/programs/promedia /countries/serbia-montenegro/media.htm.

———. 1997. *Media in the Federal Republic of Yugoslavia.* Washington, D.C.: International Research and Exchanges Board.

Soloway, Colin, and Abubaker Saddique. 2005. *An Assessment of USAID Assistance to the Radio Sector in Afghanistan.* Washington, D.C.: US Agency for International Development.

Soruco, Gonzalo, and Leonardo Ferreira. 1995. "Latin America and the Caribbean." In John C. Merrill, ed., *Global Journalism: Survey of International Communication.* White Plains, N.Y.: Longman.

Stojanovic, Svetozar. 2003. *Serbia: The Democratic Revolution*: New York: Humanity.

Strategic Marketing Media Research Institute. 2002a. *Attitudes towards and Perception of the Role of Media during the Last Months of Milosevic's Regime: Recollection Two Years After.* Belgrade: CATI Research.

———. 2002b. "Foot Soldiers." Belgrade: Otpor and CeSid.

———. 2002. *Radio, Television, and Print Research Reports.* Commissioned by International Research and Exchanges Board. Belgrade: IREX.

———. 2001. *Radio, Television, and Print Research Reports.* Commissioned by International Research and Exchanges Board. Belgrade: IREX.

———. 2000. *Radio, Television, and Print Research Reports.* Commissioned by International Research and Exchanges Board. Belgrade: IREX.

———. 1999. *Radio, Television, and Print Research Reports.* Commissioned by International Research and Exchanges Board. Belgrade: IREX.

———. 1998. *Radio, Television, and Print Research Reports.* Commissioned by International Research and Exchanges Board. Belgrade: IREX.

———. 1997. *Radio and Print Research Report.* Commissioned by International Research and Exchanges Board. Belgrade: IREX.

Taylor, Maureen. 2002. *Final Evaluation of Office of Transition Initiative's Programs in Bosnia and Croatia.* Washington, D.C.: US Agency for International Development.

Temple, Helen. 2004. *Talking Drum Sierra Leone: A Case Study.* Washington, D.C.: Management System International, US Agency for International Development.

Thompson, Mark. 1999. *Forging War: The Media in Serbia, Croatia, Bosnia, and Herzegovina.* London: University of Lutton Press.

Thompson, Mark, and Dan De Luce. 2002. "Escalating to Success? The Media Intervention in Bosnia and Herzegovina." In Monroe E. Price and Mark Thompson, eds., *Forging Peace.* Bloomington: Indiana University Press.

Timberman, David G. 2003. *Promoting Independent, Sustainable Media in Developing and Transitional Countries: The Case of Indonesia.* Washington, D.C.: US Agency for International Development.

Transparency International. 2001. "Corruption Perception Index 2001." http://www.transparency.org/documents/cpi/2001/html#cpi.

Udovicic, Radenko Dossier. 2001. "The Case of OBN: The End of the Highest Priced Media Mission in Bosnia-Herzegovina." http://archiv.medienhilfe .ch/Projecte/BiH/Mediaonline/2001-OBNcase.htm.

US Agency for International Development. 2002. "OTI Serbia and Montenegro Program Summary. http://www.usaid.gov.

———. 2002. "Serbia and Montenegro FY2000 Program Assistance to Serbia." http://www.usaid.gov.

US Department of State. 1999. "Bosnian Trust and Television News." (March 31). Washington, D.C.: Department of State.

Waisbord, Silvio. 2000. *Watchdog Journalism in South America: News, Accountability, and Democracy.* New York: Columbia University Press.

World Bank Institute. 2002. *The Right to Tell.* Washington, D.C.: World Bank.

Index

About the Book

Krishna Kumar surveys the nature and significance of international aid designed to build and strengthen independent news media in support of democratization and development. Providing the first comprehensive coverage of media assistance programs, Kumar discusses the evolution, focus, and overall impact of a range of intervention strategies. He also presents seven in-depth case studies based on extensive USAID-sponsored fieldwork; here he examines the context, accomplishments, and failures of efforts in Afghanistan, Bosnia-Herzegovina, Central America, Indonesia, Russia, Serbia, and Sierra Leone. A concluding chapter summarizes the findings of the study and suggests their important implications for international media assistance.

Krishna Kumar is senior social scientist with the US Agency for International Development. He has written or edited ten books on development, international assistance, and war-torn societies. His recent books include *Rebuilding Societies After Civil War: Critical Roles for International Assistance; Women and Civil War: Impact, Organization, and Action;* and *Postconflict Elections, Democratization, and International Assistance.*